Hey Miss

UNVEILING LEARNING'S PROMISE

Dr. Jacqueline
Mantz Rodriguez

STORIES · LESSONS · INSPIRATION

909·books

Hey Miss: Unveiling Learning's Promise
by Dr. Jacqueline Mantz Rodriguez

978-1-962702-02-7 Paperback
978-1-962702-03-4 Ebook

Library of Congress Control Number: 2025018249

909 Books Collective staff: Mark Givens and Cati Porter
Cohort One: Francesca Borella and Dr. Jacqueline Mantz Rodriguez
Edited and produced by the 909 Books Collective
Cover art by Ashley Vigil

FIRST EDITION

WWW.909BOOKS.COM

To every student, to every learner,
to every teacher, you are loved.

Para mi amiga de toda la vida, Trinidad.
You are enough.

WHAT PEOPLE ARE SAYING ABOUT

Hey Miss

Some people get lost in their wounds and failures. But Dr. Jacqueline Mantz Rodriguez has used hers to become an effective teacher, a deep listener, and a strong believer in what is possible.

Throughout the book, Dr. Mantz Rodriguez intersperses stories of students with stories from her own life. As we read these interactions, we cannot help but awaken to the opportunity we have to impact and be impacted by our encounters with others if we take the time to really listen.

—**Deborah Adele**, author of *The Yamas & Niyamas*

One of the hardest things about building relationships is the necessary truth-telling. If we are hesitant to show ourselves, warts and all, to those closest to us, consider how much more we are afraid to be ourselves in the classroom. And yet, without authenticity, we lose any connection with students. Dr. Jacqueline Mantz Rodriguez learns this on her journey to becoming her school district's Teacher of the Year. And now she brings the reader of *Hey, Miss* on that journey.

In a system that tells teachers they must control their students, Mantz Rodriguez learns the primary secret to being a great teacher is empathy. She shares her own life journey with its many setbacks including a disorderly childhood with an alcoholic parent and her own journey to sobriety. She speaks through hard-won wisdom of the power of choices that altered her life's trajectory. Her path enables her to work with students who are considered the most difficult to educate: those with learning disabilities and those who have fallen through the cracks in comprehensive high schools.

Jacqueline Mantz Rodriguez's story will inspire all readers. For those who are educators, it also offers a path to connection with students, to making a real difference in the lives of kids.

—**Victoria Waddle**, former high school English teacher, teacher-librarian, and author of *Keep Sweet*

Dr. Mantz Rodriguez's new memoir is a must read for any teacher, parent or person who cares about young people. Her deeply personal stories offer tragedy and triumph as she finds alignment with her calling, "The beauty of teaching is that every year is a new dawn..." The courageous vulnerability in sharing experiences of mistakes and challenges hits right in the feelings, while the wisdom she imparts from years of teaching pours out of the pages and will leave the reader inspired to not just support the youth but also be more gentle with themselves.

—**James Coats**, poet

Contents

Author's Note

I have been writing these stories in my head since I started teaching in 2002. What is left out of stories is important. I do not refer to any specific names of schools or districts. The names and other identifying details of all the students and many of the educators have been changed to protect their privacy. A few teachers, friends, and family members have allowed me to use their true names. These stories are from my perspective, and perspective is tricky. When writing about teaching, I sometimes get caught in moral riptides. I did my best to swim clear of them. I tried to honor the lives of the students I taught and those who taught me. It is my feathery hope that the stories within this book lead to a greater understanding of the light within us all.

My Why

> "Remember, hope is a good thing, maybe the best of things, and no good thing ever dies." —Stephen King

As I walked out of the continuation high school, I saw Ophelia in a bright pink sundress, long eyelashes, and dark curly hair standing outside the gates, texting on her phone. I smiled and waved. "Bye, Ophelia. Come to school tomorrow, okay? We need to get you caught up. Finish reading about the First Agreement."

"Hey Miss, thanks for loaning me that book to take home. I'll bring it back, I promise. I know I've been missing lots of school, but I have to take care of my sister. She's sick," Ophelia explained softly.

"What's your sister's name?" I asked.

"Paulina, but we call her Polly." Ophelia smiled, showing me a picture of a young Latina girl around eight years old with a huge smile, big brown eyes, and the same curly hair as Ophelia. "She has cancer, and my mom takes a lot of time off work, but sometimes she can't get the day off. It's hard making it to first period because I need to help her shower and feed her breakfast."

"Tell Polly she has an amazing family. Just keep talking to me, and you can work with me at lunch if needed. I'll bring those Takis I see you eating all the time," I joked.

"Thanks, Miss," replied Ophelia. "I'll bring some pozole."

"What? You know I live to eat. It's a plan," I said. Ophelia's mom drove up in a gray Honda Civic, and I waved as she got into the car. Polly waved from the back seat, holding a small stuffed animal.

I teach because of students like Ophelia. As a teacher, I have the opportunity to help change lives. Just like people helped me change my life. I want to take you back in time to a conversation with a woman I only worked with for six months, but whose words started me on the path to teaching. It is all connected. The serendipity of seemingly random events is real.

Opening a Door to the Past

"Jackie, it's been a pleasure. You've worked hard here. You were always reading a book on your breaks. I know you have support as your dad picks you up. Boy, he sure's talkative. Have you thought of going to college?" Sheriff Cagney asked me on our last day working together. She was my supervisor while I worked off my time. She was a buxom blonde with a bright smile and a no-nonsense attitude. She was friendly, but we were not friends. It was her job to oversee people on work furlough.

"I would love to go to college. I love reading books," I said.

"Think about it. You could major in literature or creative writing. I'm sure you have some stories," Sheriff Cagney said.

"That I do." I laughed, and we said our goodbyes. I never saw her again. But at that moment, I felt seen and valued by someone I respected. It renewed my self-confidence. I was more than my mistakes. I remembered that I was capable at school. A few months later, at the age of 24, I enrolled in community college and took a creative writing class, an astronomy class, and a tennis class. When I received straight A's on my report card for the first semester, I was hooked. I became addicted to the beauty of higher education. In school, unlike in life, it all made sense. I remember the first time my creative writing teacher wrote a positive note about my writing. I had written a story about my childhood cat, Greye, a Himalayan who died at seven years old. I narrated how my family did not have enough money to afford treatment for his cancer, so he was put to sleep. At the end, I told how I was still working on forgiving my mother for letting Greye die and for beating him with a broom when he peed on her bed. The professor's words on my paper infused me with warmth: "You wrote a powerful story. Keep writing. I want to read more of them." As my straight A's continued, the mistakes of my past seemed like someone else's nightmare. But we cannot pretend the past does not exist. I work on a daily basis to reframe my life with these wise words: "We will not regret the past nor wish to shut the door on it" (AA Big Book, p. 83). My past allows me to have empathy for people who have made mistakes. I believe they too can change.

There is one deep memory I choose to tell you now, once my deepest shame, now my "why." Every five years, when I renew my credential, I have to write an explanation to the Commission on Teaching Credentialing.

"At the age of twenty-four, following my misdemeanor conviction for a DUI, I made the decision to turn my life around. Since then, I have committed myself to making a positive impact on society. I am grateful for the opportunity to live a life centered on service."

It is a formality now, but when I applied the first time in 2002 for my emergency credential to teach, my hands shook as I wrote a letter of explanation:

"Teaching students with disabilities is my higher purpose, and every day I walk into the classroom is a gift. Please approve my emergency credential to teach as this is how I give back to society. I thank you in advance for seeing that people can change if given the opportunity."

My emergency teaching credential application was approved. How did it feel to receive a chance to rebuild my life? It felt miraculous. Teaching allowed me to work with young people who reminded me of myself. Teaching gave me hope—hope that I could do better and be better. It helped me become the woman I am today, the one writing this book. The woman who loves herself, cracks and all, as they are why my light shines so bright from within.

My self-destructive path started during my teenage years when I spiraled into alcoholism. At age twenty-four, I got pulled over while drinking and driving. I was arrested and stayed in jail because I had warrants for driving on a suspended license. When I went to court, I told the judge, "Do whatever you want with me. I don't care," and pleaded guilty. The judge said, "For the D.U.I., I am sentencing you to 120 days. Also, for the first warrant 120 days, and for the second warrant 120 days. These will all run consecutively for a total of 360 days in jail, Ms. Mantz. Maybe this time will help you reflect on how you endangered the lives of others with your actions." Often, sentencing runs concurrent. But not in this case. I was sentenced to serve out my time at the Sybil Brand Institution, a jail in City Terrace, Los Angeles County, California.

After court, I was handcuffed and transferred to a bus that transported inmates to Sybil Brand. The jail was built in 1963 and closed in 1997, a few years after I was there. My memories are gray, but I recall the bologna sandwiches on pasty white bread they gave us to eat. I ate the sandwich. I could always eat. They searched me but not like in the movies. The way the female guards made sure you were not "holding" anything in an orifice was methodical. I received an orange jumpsuit, off-white granny panties, a utilitarian bra, black canvas shoes, a plastic comb, a mini toothbrush, toothpaste, and a thin blanket. I had looked up pictures of Sybil Brand's interior on the internet, and there seemed to be cells, but I was not in a cell. I was housed in a dormitory-style room with rows of cots. I was desperate the first few days.

The women at Sybil Brand were kind to me. One woman with bronzed skin and thick plaited braids saw me sitting on my cot, clutching my meager belongings. “I'm Serena. Just relax, honey. Lunchtime is soon. Take a nap. I have a book if you want to read something.” I borrowed her book and read lying on my stomach on the upper cot. Later in the day that went on forever, someone wheeled around a mini-library, just like Brooks did in one of my favorite movies, *The Shawshank Redemption.* I checked out books from the mobile cart and borrowed books from other women in my row. I read to lose myself in stories and to avoid replaying the horrible decisions I had made that sent me to jail.

“What are you reading that keeps you so quiet, girl?” my cot neighbor asked.

“I'm rereading *Charlotte's Web* by E. B. White. It's about a pig named Wilbur and his best friend, a spider named Charlotte.” I marked my page with my black plastic comb.

“Was that a movie? I remember it. Can you read me a few pages?” she asked.

“Sure, if you tell me your name,” I said with a smile. “I have to warn you, I do funny voices.”

“That's cool. It's Latasha. What's yours?”

“Jackie, nice to meet you,” I said and began reading. “Chapter one is titled ‘Before Breakfast.’ ‘Where's Papa going with that ax?’ said Fern to her mother as they were setting the table for breakfast...” (White, pg.1). Latasha jumped up when I shrieked, “You mean kill it? Just because it's smaller than the others?”

We ended up reading a chapter a night, and she taught me how to play King's Corners and Spades. I taught her how to play Rummy. "You sure do read well. Do you have kids or work with them?" Latasha asked.

"I don't have any kids, but I tutored some students in special education in high school. It was a lot of fun."

"Something to think about. I love hearing you read to me," Latasha said.

A young woman named Lupe knew how to play Rummy too, and we would all sit on my cot playing to five hundred points. I won a lot. My dad played Rummy with my sisters and me when we were little. Serena, Latasha, and Lupe were but a few of the women I remember. I want you all to see these women and feel their humanity. We would all go to sleep in long rows of cots, and the ladies would say goodnight to one another. "Good night, Jackie." "Good night, Latasha." "Good night, Lupe." "Good night!" I felt like John-Boy in the television show *The Waltons*. I got to know many women in the time I spent at Sybil Brand. I told many my story, and they would often shake their heads when I said I declined a public defender and asked to be sentenced.

"Never do that again," they chastised.

"I don't intend to ever go back to jail," I replied.

I remember how women shook and shivered in their cots, their thin beige blankets covering their forms. "They're kicking heroin, leave them alone," said Lupe. There was a sense of camaraderie while I was in jail. We would share the snacks we bought at the commissary in the evening, and we would let out a collective groan when the smell of corn nuts would waft over to our row.

"I can't wait to get back to my kids," Latasha said. "My girl is graduating high school in June. She's smarter than her mama. Are you married?"

"No, I have a boyfriend, though. I can't wait to see my family. I have an identical twin sister," I explained. Many women spoke of their children. They hoped to get out so they could raise their kids and be with their families.

There were moments of almost normalcy within the concrete walls. One night, there was an ad-lib talent contest in the rec room. At the same time the televisions were blaring images of O.J. Simpson's car chase on the small screens above, we sang and performed for one another. I gulped down my fear, asked a few friends to serve as back-up dancers, and sang out a cappella, "At first I was afraid, I was petrified..." The back-up dancers waved their hands back and forth to my almost on-key singing, and I smiled as if I was at a karaoke contest, except I didn't have a drink in each hand.

The guards frightened me the most. Their inhumanity and indifference to the scale of suffering opened my eyes and rocked me to the depths of my core. It was the way they just glanced over you as if you were nothing. I remember walking past the bathroom in my orange jumpsuit. Guards had the door open, and I saw the body of a young woman lying on the floor. She was prone and her neck was at an odd angle. Was she dead? I learned to swallow questions after I saw that people who questioned or argued were led away to solitary confinement. We were just numbers and statistics. This was another lesson I learned. I needed to change my life. I never wanted to be at the mercy of the system again.

I also learned I was not meant to live in a cage. My feathers were too bright, and I could not bear to live a life without my family and friends. One night, I prayed on my knees with all my Catholic childhood faith in God for grace and mercy.

"I will do better, be better, and help others if you help me, God, get through this time safely." A miracle occurred. It had only been two weeks, and I was released to work off the rest of my time on work furlough.

Recently, I asked my mom about this time, and she did not remember much about it. Juanita, my twin, remembers it vividly, her public-defender side bristling. "Mom went and talked to someone down at the jail. She may not remember, but I do. You were stupid to do what you did, but it worked out. You were in jail for two weeks, did six months on work furlough, didn't get on probation, and you had no fines to pay."

As a woman in my fifties now, I understand the severity of my behavior. In *The Shawshank Redemption*, Red tells the parole board, "I look back on the way I was then: a young, stupid kid... I want to talk to him. I want to try to talk some sense to him, tell him the way things are." This is why I teach. I am writing this right now so I may unlearn fear and shame. With students, I talk about the power of our choices. Our lives are fragile, woven into form by our decisions.

The morning of my release, when I saw my dad's faded burgundy Beretta pull up, I looked up into the bluest sky and mouthed, "Thank you, God." Then, I ran into my dad's arms, and he hugged me tight and said, "Are you hungry?" We drove to McDonald's right off the I-10. I always look at those specific golden arches and remember. Those two cheeseburgers with extra pickles, fresh fries, and a large Diet Coke with extra ice sipped out of that thick plastic straw was the best meal of my life.

I felt grateful for having my family's support while I strove to rebuild my life. For the next six months, I worked at the Pomona Courthouse and lived with my parents. My father would drop me off in the morning and then drive me to my other job in the evening. I promised myself that I would make my mother and father proud by serving my time at the courthouse with a positive attitude.

This time in my life has influenced how I work with young people who are experiencing challenges. I won't give up on them. It is one way to pay forward my family's love and support. I know most young people want to do well in life and be well; they just don't know what they don't know. I try to help them find their path to hope. Maybe I give them a snack or listen to them when they are having a hard day. Or I might work with them one-on-one on a paper for my class or even on assignments from other teachers. I try to give them what they need, not what I think they need.

It was through work furlough at the Pomona Courthouse that I met Sheriff Cagney.

"As long as you do your work and stay out of trouble here, we will get along fine," she said to me on my first day. I arrived at 8 a.m. and worked until 3 p.m. On my breaks, I ate my bagged lunch and read a book I had brought from home. We had plenty of books lying around at my parents' house, mostly Harlequin romance novels. I worked off my time by cleaning and following directions. I stayed to myself. My co-workers were apt to hide and do "other activities" while working off their time. All I wanted to do was finish up this period of my life.

After I finished my work furlough, I started going to Chaffey College in Rancho Cucamonga. From there, I went to San Bernardino Valley College, and two years later, received my Associate of Arts degree. Then, I transferred to California State University, San Bernardino, and received my Bachelor of Arts degree in English (with honors), and found teaching. God knew that teaching is an act of love, and by learning to teach and love my students, I would eventually become teachable myself. The promise I made to God has sustained me for the last twenty-plus years of teaching. Now, I want to tell you more stories, as it is through stories that we learn.

It's All About Relationships

My path as a teacher started with a friendship. More than twenty-five years ago, my friend Melody and I met at San Bernardino Valley College. She had a serious face and a caring soul. We met in sociology class. Melody majored in sociology although she ended up becoming a special education teacher. During those years, she was a close friend. We both transferred and graduated from California State University, San Bernardino. After we graduated in 2001, she started teaching at a non-public school near Colton, California. Non-public schools are private schools certified by the California Department of Education to provide educational placement and services to students with special education needs that go beyond the capabilities of a public-school setting. They are not very common now, but back then, many school districts placed students who were a danger to themselves or others in these types of placements.

Melody and I caught up one day when we met for lunch on the weekend. As we dipped our bread sticks into Alfredo sauce and ate our bottomless salads at The Olive Garden, Melody told me about teaching special education students and invited me to take a tour of the campus. I had had memorable experiences with kids with special needs in high school and at work, so I agreed to visit the next week. I was managing a team at a call center at the time, but struggled when I had to fire people. The corporation did not care if a mom had a sick kid and no child-care. Corporate management was not for me.

When I walked into the non-public school to visit Melody, I

saw a gray room with foam padding on all the walls.

"What is that room?" I asked Melody as she walked me around the small campus.

"It's a rubber room," she said with a grimace and a shake of her head.

"What's a rubber room?"

"It's a room the kids go into when they are escalated," Melody explained. "It's frightening when some of these kids get upset." As of 2019, seclusion or behavioral restraint may be used "only to control behavior that poses a clear and present danger of serious physical harm to the pupil or others that cannot be immediately prevented by a response that is less restrictive" (Education Code Section 49005.4).

We walked around the campus, and then Melody went into her classroom. I waved to a man with silver hair and kind eyes wearing sneakers with his school polo and khakis. He said, "Hello, I'm Dr. Bob, the campus director. You have such a nice smile, Jackie. I see you're visiting Melody. Where do you teach?"

"I'm not a teacher, but I manage a team at INFONXX. I also waitress part-time."

"Have you ever thought of working with kids?"

"I don't have a teaching credential."

"You have a degree?"

"Yes, in English."

"Let's go talk in my office. We're always looking for people to teach kids, and I have an opening for a substitute in Barstow."

"Umm, that's a long drive from my house in Ontario."

"Oh, you live in Ontario, good to know as we have a campus in Rancho Cucamonga."

My teaching career was launched. During the day, I taught out in Barstow and went to work right after, managing the night shift of customer service representatives in Riverside. After I almost fell asleep driving home one night, I knew I had to choose. I struggled financially on a beginning teacher's salary ($29,000), so I continued waitressing part-time on the weekends.

What was the draw of teaching? Well, the first day was like nothing I had ever experienced before. When I pulled up to the desert campus surrounded by barbed wire, I gulped. There were kids playing basketball on the court. An Opie Taylor-looking kid paced back and forth along the fence. I got out of my car, and Opie ran to the gate and threw a big rock over the fence. *Plunk* went the rock right on the hood of my shiny forest green Mazda Miata. I shook my head. Did this just happen? I shrugged, went up to the entrance of the gate, showed my driver's license to the security guard, and walked to the campus office. I introduced myself to the director's secretary.

"Hi, my name's Jackie Mantz. I'm here to substitute for the next few weeks. Some kid just threw a big rock at my car and dented it?"

"Park further away from the gate," she said. This would be a foreshadowing of education's unique way of dealing with issues within the system, but I didn't see it then. I shrugged and parked far away from the gate. That dent was still there when I traded the car in a few years later. I worked at a non-public school for two years. Teaching gave me a reason to get up in the morning, not take that first drink, and to care about others.

My first few years of teaching were extremely difficult. Teachers are always on stage, and it is exhausting. But, after a few years, you get used to it, and this is when the magic begins to happen. I always tell new teachers, "Learning to be a good teacher takes time. You need to learn what works for you. But if you have an excellent work ethic and a loving heart for kids, you can become great. Oh, and you're not their friend." You must have boundaries as teachers are mandated reporters. Also, kids don't follow the norms of a class for their friend; they follow the class norms because they respect a teacher who has taught them the expectations over and over again—verbally, visually, and by modeling them. The teacher must lead by example. The "Do as I say, not as I do" rule fails epically in classrooms across the world. Students can smell a fake and, like bees, they can smell fear too. Teachers are social workers, therapists, and even second parents. It is important to do everything we can for kids. I learned to love and work hard for people from my dad and mom.

My dad, John William Mantz, Jr., was born in Great Falls, Montana during the depression. His parents put him and his siblings into an orphanage for a short time, as they could not afford to feed them because of their drinking habits. At the orphanage, my dad was fed a lot of white rice with poured grease over toast. To the day he died, Daddy hated white rice. But he loved to cook and feed people, especially home baked bread.

"Never go to bed hungry or angry. Always kiss the ones you love goodnight," Daddy would say. If Daddy's legacy was love and nurturing, my mother, Juliana Coltilde Uriarte Mantz, bequeathed to me a work ethic of excellent proportions. My mom worked all her life, mostly as a waitress, until the age of sixty-nine. For many years, she toiled at two jobs. I worked with her at some of the restaurants. She knew her trade, and she had trained me well.

Great waitresses should be teachers. I've said it a lot that all my years of hard work as a waitress prepared me for the rigors of teaching. As a teacher, I believe deeply that one must love and understand students. Yet, love is not enough. When you love someone, you work your butt off for them. You teach them how to work hard for themselves too. Like my mom told me at my first job at the Olympic Flame in Pomona, "If you can lean, you can clean."

My mom was married before she met my dad and had a son, David, who was born deaf. To provide David with better educational opportunities, she moved to Oregon where he attended a boarding school for the deaf. She worked at a laundromat during the week and brought David home with her on the weekends. One night when my mom was walking with him, tragedy happened in an instant. He broke away from her and ran into the street. He was struck and killed by a car as my mom lunged for him. David was five years old. She still mourns for the life that might have been since his passing in 1969, two years before Juanita and I were born. I got to know him through the stories my mom told me about his antics.

"He tore up all my money in my wallet once. I was so mad, Jackie. I was hard on him. I didn't know how to raise a deaf child. I did my best," she said.

I think of David and all the students I've had the privilege to teach, and all the magnificent teachers who have paved the way before me and those who will come after. This book is for all of us, illustrating the South African word *ubuntu*— which means, "I am because we are." We are all connected, and our humanity and compassion is what binds us together as a community.

Filling in the Gaps

Gap One

Should I fill in the gaps? Should I share details of my private life? This is a book about teaching, but teachers are more than educators; we are fully fleshed-out individuals. While I love puppets and use them in my teaching daily, we teachers are not mere puppets ourselves. We don't reside in school closets, only emerging when class begins. So, I will fill in the gaps just enough. What we choose to leave out of a memoir is just as important as what we include.

We all have had relationships in life that have not been successful. A former long-time boyfriend had stood by me through the D.U.I., but I couldn't get sober for him just because he wanted me to. I had to do it for myself. He contributed so much to my life, and I want to acknowledge the gifts of that relationship:

Thank you for tutoring me in math. Your strong, caring family supported me through my B.A. degree. I am deeply sorry for hurting you all those years ago. You were my best friend.

Non-Public School Years

The non-public school eventually transferred me to the Rancho Cucamonga campus, where I would become a full-time teacher. Teaching mirrored my childhood in many ways—it was chaotic and always an adventure. The students were grappling with their issues. All students at the school qualified for special education services under the qualifying disability, Emotional Disturbance (ED). Students with ED have learning difficulties. They have a challenging time forming and maintaining relationships with others, may display inappropriate behavior or feelings in normal situations, and can have pervasive unhappiness or depression. Some students have physical symptoms or fears related to peers, staff, or school. This condition does include schizophrenia (34 CFR Sec. 300.8(c)(4)). Essentially, our students faced major difficulties with both their behavior and mental health.

The paraeducator, Kaylee, taught the class before me and was used to doing things her way. She exuded pure bravado with her dark, straight, flat-ironed hair, caramel skin, and confident attitude. For those unfamiliar with education, paraeducators provide instructional support under a teacher's supervision. They are also known as teacher's aides or assistants.

"So, I've got another one, huh? The last teacher only lasted a month. What's your name?" she asked me, her hand on her hip and her eyebrows raised. I smiled, trying not to stare at her rhinestone belt with the big "K" belt buckle.

"I'm Jackie. It's going to be great working with you," I said.

Kaylee had a close rapport with the students, more akin to a friend than a teacher. But Kaylee had "game." The kids were drawn to her self-confidence, always begging her to play basketball at recess and vying to sit beside her during lunch at the picnic tables. They listened to her. She didn't always listen to me, though, and I wondered if we would get along, at least for the kids' sake. As the paraeducator, Kaylee had been teaching the class as substitute after substitute drifted in and out. I didn't know this at the time, but special education teacher vacancies are hard to fill, especially teachers who work with students with emotional disturbances. "Ms. Jackie, you mean we gotta read this story, answer questions, and write about it? We never had to do this with Ms. Kaylee." She stood at the back of the class, smiling.

"You do what Ms. Jackie says, even if it's a lot of work," Kaylee interjected. This was my first experience working with a paraeducator, so at first, if she gave me attitude, I would give it back.

"Are you trying to tell me something, Ms. Kaylee?" I asked.

"No, I was trying to compliment you," she retorted.

"Uh oh, Ms. Kaylee and Ms. Jackie are going to go at it," the class murmured. I had enough sense at that moment to step back. This was not going well.

"Kaylee, could we split the kids up and work with them in small groups on the story? I need your help," I suggested. We had reached an understanding; both of us wanted what was best for the kids. I encouraged her to read with the kids and modeled writing responses, demonstrating how to construct paragraphs. Kaylee took copious notes during these times. It took a few weeks, but one day when we broke into groups, I saw her demonstrating to the kids how to write a simple sentence.

"Remember, like Ms. Jackie told you, always start a new sentence with a capital and end it with a period. Now, this is the confusing part—it's not always a period. Yup, we have those question marks and exclamation points. Man, I should always end my dialogue with an exclamation point, ya know!"

One day she complimented me: "You teach all right, Ms. Jackie. You know your books and how to get the kids to write."

"Ms. Kaylee, you have a way with the kids. I admire your connections with them," I responded.

"I was one of these kids. Why do you think I work here? It ain't for the pay." She walked to her purse to get more pink bubble gum, which she loved popping in class as she worked. She also worked nights at a group home, where Billy, one of the kids in our elementary class, stayed. He always stood by Kaylee wherever we were out at recess or lunch together, with his red hair, green eyes, chapped lips, and ill-fitting clothes.

"I work at the group home where Billy stays," Kaylee informed me while munching on an apple. "They feed them crap. Sometimes the bread has mold on it." Now, I understood why she had brought an extra sandwich and handed it to Billy when he left on the bus. Reflecting on those years, I realized I was operating on instinct. I didn't particularly like Kaylee; she could be rude on some days. But I knew we had to work together. Most teachers, including me, don't know what they're doing in the first few years. It's disorienting. You have to perform too. If you can't, the kids know it. So, I emulated what I had seen other teachers do in classes, but I had also learned what not to do by watching others. I stayed at the non-public school for two years. Kaylee and I were never friends, but we became friendly. I often wonder where Kaylee is now.

There were many interesting characters at this school, like Matt, who taught in the classroom next door. Matt was a young fifty with an easy smile, charm galore, and a love of reading the newspaper with his feet propped up on a small footstool. Matt didn't teach; he photocopied. He handed kids packets of math problems for them to wade through.

"I know addition and subtraction, Mr. Matt."

"Do it anyway. Fractions are tomorrow."

"I know that too."

"Good, you'll pass my class then."

Matt also taught science. There was a student in his class nicknamed "Cowboy" due to the rodeo belt buckle he wore along with a cream-colored Stetson. Cowboy liked to think he knew a lot about science. He told Mr. Matt he wanted to teach the class. So he did. I walked into the classroom to borrow some pencils, and Cowboy was teaching the class about spiders. Cowboy drew a spider and began diagramming it.

"Don't spiders have eight legs?" I asked.

"Oh yeah, right." Cowboy added two legs to the diagram. Mr. Matt glanced up from his newspaper, smiled, and shook his head.

"Cowboy, can you also add the spinnerets on the spider's head?" Mr. Matt said as he got up and passed out spider diagrams to the class. Mr. Matt and I talked about our differing philosophies. He was a veteran and had worked in many special education settings.

"Jackie, I appreciate what you're trying to do with these kids," he said as he munched on a sandwich in our breakroom.

"But you know they're only going to retain so much information. They're on medication and have a lot of other stuff going on, so I try to make my classroom a chill place."

"But, we have some smart kids here, Matt. They can do a lot more than we're giving them," I argued, my voice raising an octave.

"Sure, but where's our curriculum? Do you know how much this school is making off these kids daily? Yet, I don't have higher level math or science books, so I do what I can. I've taught in public school in special ed classes too, and it wasn't much better. They are the misfits, the other kids. So, I do what I do. The kids like my class. That's enough for me. Let's see if you are going to the library every evening after you have been doing this for twenty years."

"Matt, you have a point with the curriculum. It's frustrating," I replied and walked back to my classroom as the bell had rung. Our conversation planted seeds of doubt within me about the ethical ramifications of a for-profit school serving students with disabilities. This eventually led me to question if this school was the right fit for me.

As the only high school English teacher at the non-public school, the only textbooks I had were archaic grammar books that were written in and a box of SRA (Science Reading Associates) materials that were leveled for readers. For the higher-level readers, the curriculum was below their reading level and only focused on foundational skills. Many nights after school, I would go to the Ontario City Library and check out novels, short stories, and poetry collections. I would then photocopy my favorite excerpts, read the material, and create questions for them to answer as well as writing assignments related to the readings. It worked. My kids enjoyed reading higher-level literature as most of them were highly intelligent and excellent readers. We had lots of loud conversations about stories and poetry. My first year teaching high school consisted of the following: an excerpt from *The Color Purple*, poetry by Robert Frost and Emily Dickinson, the novels *Of Mice and Men* and *The House on Mango Street*. I also threw in some short stories by Edgar Allan Poe and Stephen King. The kids loved the macabre.

As a veteran teacher, I know students are required to have textbooks per the landmark Williams case in 2004. Back then, in 2002, I accepted whatever people gave me. If there was no appropriate grade-level curriculum, then I thought it was my job to find one. Now that I've been a teacher for twenty-plus years, I no longer spend my evenings photocopying materials at the public library. Fortunately, we now have the internet, and I have a wealth of curricula at my fingertips. Technology has changed and continues to change the way we teach. There will always be new technology like ChatGPT. It's important that teachers guide students on using Artificial Intelligence ethically and to promote honesty in their work. Education is part science and part art. One must teach the standards, but one has to do it in a way that resonates with students.

Every class is different. Some students love talking to one another. Other classes like working independently. What will work with one student or class may not work with another student or class. Teachers have to have a bag of tricks to pull from once they get to know their students. And don't forget about love. Teaching day in and day out is an act of love. If you don't love teaching, you are in the wrong profession. Students remember their worst teachers just as they remember the ones who made a positive difference in their lives.

The years I spent in such a restrictive setting still influences my teaching today. The canon of literature is used throughout high school English classes. I use modern work by writers of color who have been published within the last twenty years. I still use some "classics," such as *The Four Agreements*, *The Handmaid's Tale*, and *The House on Mango Street*, but I am always on the lookout for new books that capture the lived experiences of people who look like our students. It is also important that the books are written by people who look like them too.

Back to the non-public school years: Even then, I enjoyed teaching writing.

"Can we write our own poems based on 'Hope is the Thing with Feathers'?" asked Dora.

"Do you like poetry, Dora?" I asked.

"My whole life is a poem, Ms. Jackie," Dora said. She wasn't joking. Her poetry was dark and imagery laden. She wrote about suicide, molestation, and cutting. Her arms were covered in scars. I encouraged her to write. Teaching at this school taught me to support what people today now call "the whole child." Dora was trying to get off drugs. With her mom's and with the school's permission, I was allowed to take her to her first Narcotics Anonymous meeting. This would not happen today, but it worked.

On June 9th, 2024, I received a Facebook message from Dora:

> *Hey Jackie, thank you for taking me under your wing in high school. I'm sorry for any pain I caused you. I have so much love for you sister* 🖤 *. I hope life is treating you well.*

I replied: "Dora, you are a gift. I am glad you are doing well.

I'm sober fourteen years, remarried, and still teaching. Life is good. I'm grateful you were my student. You taught me how brilliant students can be despite their challenges. You are loved."

She wrote back: "14 years? Wow, that's amazing. My sobriety date is April 16th of this year."

I replied, "We only have today."

It is my hope that Dora can visit me someday in the Coachella Valley. She is in her thirties now and doing well.

One of the goals of public education is to help students grow into productive members of society who live independent lives. Students' mental health in the United States is a serious issue. Back then, students like Dora with mental health issues were put in schools such as the one I've been describing. Today, I believe Dora would have received the mental health support she needed to stay in a comprehensive high school program. Despite being highly gifted academically, Dora did not go to college. Very few students with the qualifying disability of emotional disturbance have gone on to postsecondary education (Wynne, M. E., Ausikaitis, A. E., & Satchwell, M., 2013) because their mental health impacts their ability to access learning. They may also be placed in a special education setting. Historically, students in special education have lower academic outcomes than their general education peers. Dora graduated from high school and participated in a poetry program in Los Angeles, her hometown.

During that first year at the non-public school, I checked out Shakespeare's *Hamlet* from the library, and the highest reading group read and performed it aloud in class. They were so exceptional that we ended up performing it at the church across the street. I persuaded the ruddy-faced priest into letting us use it on a weekday, employing all the Catholic school charm I could muster. The kids got into it, learning their lines and acting out the play. We designed sets and created costumes from the local thrift store. CB, a student with autism blessed with an incredible memory, played Hamlet. He arrived at school every day dressed in all black, a velvet purple cape, and heavy black eyeliner. The day before the performance, I offered him a copy of his photocopied lines, but he politely declined, saying, "No thank you, Ms. Jackie." Then he pulled out a skull from his backpack and walked to the front of the class.

"To be, or not to be, that is the question: Whether 'tis nobler in the mind to suffer the slings and arrows of outrageous fortune, Or to take arms against a sea of troubles and by opposing end them. To die—to sleep..." said CB in a loud, deep voice. He recited the entire soliloquy. I was so surprised I forgot to clap. But the class applauded, and I joined in, still in a daze.

"That'll do, CB, that'll do," I said softly after he sat down next to me. At the end of the performance at the church, the cast received standing ovations from the parents and staff. I cried. I did not know these kids were supposed to fail; hence, the power of the self-fulfilling prophecy. I saw them as capable, and hence they acted capable. It was my first huge moment in teaching. These were the kids that society had labeled as dangerous and determined that they needed to be institutionalized. Yet, they wanted to learn. In fact, they were desperate to learn. After that performance, I knew I was meant to teach.

Back then, all you needed was a degree, and you could get an emergency credential. After that, you would have five years to complete your preliminary teaching credential. Becoming a teacher put me on a lifelong education track. I never do things halfway. The teaching part at the non-public school was challenging. Many of the students came from traumatic backgrounds. I got it; they were angry and upset, so I did my best to stay calm and work with them, and try to teach them something they wanted to learn.

The school focused on basic academics as well as behavior. On Fridays, we would take students who had earned top-tier status for excellent behavior on community outings. We visited the mall in Halloween costumes. I dressed up as Robin of Batman fame because Eminem had a video dressed up as the character at the time. We stopped doing mall visits, though, when kids were caught shoplifting.

On another of our outings, we took the kids to the ice-skating rink. On the drive to the rink, Jared, the driver, and campus security asked the kids, "Who knows how to ice skate?" No one raised their hands. CB, Dora, and Billy were all on the trip. The rest of the students were in the elementary teacher Joy's class. At the rink, I watched them tie up their white skates and walk onto the ice. There was no way I was going out there as I was born a klutz.

"Man, those blades look sharp," I said to myself. Billy, Dora, and CB hooked arms, laughing as they slowly moved along the ice. I looked away for a second, and when I looked back, they were a tangle of arms and legs, and there was blood pooling on the ice. Jared and I ran onto the ice. The manager came up and shook his head.

"We've called an ambulance. That kid's leg is going to need stitches." Dora's skate had sliced open Billy's leg. What were we thinking, taking these kids ice skating? I rode in the ambulance with Billy and waited for his group home manager to arrive at the hospital.

"What did you do this time, Billy?" Those were the first words the manager Dick said when we walked into the room. It said a lot about the environment Billy lived in at his group home.

Another outing I still remember clearly is our trip to the local community college. It highlights the gifts and challenges of the students we were responsible for educating while they were with us. CB immediately endeared himself to me with his hard work and deadpan sense of humor. He always wore black shirts and pants, and his mom ensured that his Afro was properly cut and shaped, though CB dreamed of letting it grow freely. "I'm going for that Chia Pet look, Ms. Jackie, but my mom keeps taking me to the barber," he would joke, always eliciting a laugh.

CB had an above-average intelligence; he was on the autism spectrum and had other mental health issues. He would escape from his house in the middle of the night to go to 7-Eleven, even with his mother sleeping near the front door. While generally chill, CB could be violent in class. The students enjoyed teasing him by stealing his meticulously completed work. To help him focus, I started giving CB independent reading books during class. I would read a book checked out from the Upland Public Library and then pass it on to him. CB read every book by my favorite writer at the time, Anne Rice. He loved all things goth and painted his nails black, and he wrote meticulous book reports on all his readings, detailing the plot, characters, setting, and theme. It seemed like a way for him to escape the world. CB was as peaceful as Walden Pond when he read or wrote. There were other highly intelligent students, but none as hardworking as CB.

Dr. Jess, the campus director, wore her blond hair down, large hoop earrings, and was as bossy as she was stylish.

"So, we need to plan a field trip. Let's go to Chaffey College since it's right up the street. Ms. Jackie, you can chaperone with me, considering you were a student there," she declared.

"Any student in the high school class can attend as long as they behave appropriately next week and get their permission slips signed," she added. With only seventy students in the entire school, and ten in high school at that, seven out of the ten qualified to go. However, the morning of the trip, CB wasn't there when we loaded up the van to leave.

Jared drove the van while Dr. Jess and I sat with the students. It only took twenty minutes to reach Chaffey College. When we arrived at the parking lot for the student services offices, CB was standing there, dressed in black slacks and a green sweater, holding a notebook. We parked, got out, and CB approached us.

"So, I took the bus from my house. I looked up the route. You said if we had a permission slip, we could go," he stated matter-of-factly. Unfortunately, I had bad news. He began to pace in circles after learning he couldn't join the Chaffey tour; he was technically absent since he didn't arrive at school and ride in the van with us.

"My mom couldn't bring me to school today, and she told me to stay home, but I had the college field trip. I want to go here after high school," he said in a flat voice, twisting his fingers around each other as he spoke.

"We'll call your mom to come pick you up," Dr. Jess told him. If she hadn't been there, I might have allowed CB to do the tour. He looked at her, dropped his notebook, and ran. Jared, who also served as the crisis counselor, chased after him with a walkie-talkie radio in hand.

While CB and Jared played tag, the rest of the students and I visited Student Services. They took us on a tour of the campus and answered questions about the school's admission process. We ate lunch in their cafeteria and finished our tour at the library. At that moment, I wished for CB to be standing beside me. His mom picked him up that day, and he came back to school the next day with a grudge against Dr. Jess, telling me, "All she had to do was let me stay." I secretly agreed. I know Dr. Jess was following the "rules," but if possible, we need to take into account our students' needs. She could have called his mom and had her chaperone. There is a lot of inflexibility in the education system. This is one reason I cannot be an administrator. We are sometimes limited by the constraints of the system in which we work.

I made strong connections with many students, but I didn't get along with others due to my bias. When I started teaching, I judged kids by their clothes. My mother's voice would echo in my ears: "Don't hang out with cholos, Jackie. You will end up in prison. Take off those Dickies and that white tank top."

During my first year of teaching at the non-public school, I looked at my student Carlos and only saw his clothing: tan Dickies and a gray Pendleton. His black hair was greased back, and he wore black flat shoes.

"Does Ms. Mantz think she's better than us? That fat bitch is brown too," Carlos said one time I was standing nearby during lunch. All I heard was the fat remark. Kids can feel it when you judge them. I never got to know Carlos, and he never did any work with me. I regret the way I treated him. But we all make mistakes as teachers. There was too much going on some days. I forgot to listen more than I spoke. In the early days, I was harsh with kids rather than forgiving. I needed to be an amalgamation of my father and my mother when I taught. Daddy was unconditional love. Mom had an unwavering work ethic.

The curse and gift of teaching is that there are always multiple new endings, beginnings, and opportunities to learn from mistakes. We do not know people's stories. If we build trust and community in our classroom, they may tell us, but not always.

I taught at the non-public school for two years, but the long hours, low pay, lack of educational materials, and stressful days made me yearn for a more supportive teaching environment. Melody, who had helped me get the job, left to teach elementary for a local school district.

Now, I will tell you a story from my teenage years, so you understand more about my why. Please have grace and forgiveness for my mom and me. She is one of the reasons I am alive today. I tell this story not to sensationalize or punish but to educate. We are all suffering. We need to accept people where they are, not where we want them to be. Every student and family has a story. When they walk into our classrooms, we do not know what they have been through the morning or night before.

Shower Cuffs

Harsh beads rained down on me in the shower. I planned my escape as I scrubbed, planned and seethed. It was already 9 p.m. on a Saturday night; I was sixteen, had my own car, and was off from my job at Sbarro's Pizza. I was ready to go party at the kegger of the year. Juanita, my twin, had already taken off with her best friend, Michelle. But a few minutes before, I had been making out with my boyfriend, Chris, in my bedroom when my mom walked into my room. Chris and I jumped up and my mom yelled, "Get him the hell out of here." She worked long hours as a waitress to help support our family. Daddy had struggled with his physical and mental health since the death of my half-sister Barbara, my dad's daughter from his previous marriage. She had died suddenly in a car accident related to alcohol.

Everyone in our crew knew of my mom. She was a legend. Wherever we went, people talked about Mom's notorious temper. It was almost funny, if you didn't have to live it. Lately, partying and sex seemed safer than being home.

"I think you should just leave with me, Jackie," Chris said. "Your mom is pissed. Seriously dude, she is like hella mad. I wouldn't even shower."

"I'm just going to shower, talk to Annie, and change quickly. I will meet you at your house." Chris was outta there. I walked into my little sister's room where she and Paula were dressed up as journalists. They had my dad's checkered blazers on, fedora-like hats, and each held a pad of paper in their hand.

"Can we go to the party and interview people?" asked Paula.

"Yeah, we want to ask them when was the last time they ate a hot dog. Mom said you just ate one and she is going to make you throw it up," teased Annie.

"Nope, I'm out. You two need to stay out of Mom's way tonight. She is in a mood," I warned them.

"Paula and I are going to hang out in our secret place," said Annie. Before I got in the shower, I laid out my new yellow, low-cut shirt from Contempo, a tight black skirt, and black boots. I rummaged through my jewelry box and threw huge cross earrings and a handful of black plastic bracelets on the counter. As the hot water plummeted down upon me, I thought about the bottle of Strawberry Hill Chris had waiting for me. Suddenly, a hand pulled my hair and me with it, naked, out of the shower. Words and hands now hit at my bright red skin. I did not cry. I just tried to hold my own rage amid the words and the pain to my pride.

"No daughter of mine is going to be doing this shit in my home." Time stopped then. I had hit her back for the first time. She looked at me in shock and left the room. I grabbed a towel and crumpled against the bathroom door and let the tears come. I cried until I was slumped over in exhaustion. I stood when I heard a firm knock on the door. When I opened it, I saw an older female police officer looking grimly at me still in the towel.

"I need you to come out here and talk to us. Your mom says you hit her," the police officer said sternly.

"Can I get dressed?"

"No, just come downstairs with us. We need to talk to you and your mom."

I felt small and dirty. But I forced myself to go downstairs and sit in a chair with my legs pushed together, still in my small, blue-and-white striped towel. My hair was wet and dripping down my cheeks. I did not look at my mom. She was uttering a litany of my extracurricular activities, most of them true.

"Ma'am, we can teach her a lesson and take her down to the station if you want. She might need a night in jail," said the female police officer. Her partner appraised me, and I could feel his eyes on my legs and the line between my breasts. Tears fell upon my cheeks. I was ashamed. My eyes were downcast, and my mouth quivered. Just then Daddy walked in the door. He had on his work jeans and a khaki green, collared shirt with the Mayflower logo on it. He looked tired but was smoking a cigarette and holding a six pack of Budweiser. He glanced at the police, at my mom, and at the police again in disbelief. Luckily, he had not been drinking, yet. He already had one "wet reckless" on his license.

"Officers, what's going on?" Daddy asked.

They told him. He looked at me, and our eyes locked. He took a deep breath and sighed.

"Judy, I need to talk to you," he said to Mom. They went into the kitchen and talked. We all heard Mom's raised voice and the door slam. My mom was now speeding away to Orange County.

"I will deal with my daughter, officers," said Daddy. "Thank you for coming."

The officers looked at each other, shrugged their shoulders, and nodded. They left us to our peace after the chaos. I knew even then that this act would cost my father dearly. Daddy suffered a lot in life, but his heart was huge and his smile wide. He smiled through life even amid the pain. I take after him, I suppose.

On Monday, I went to school. I sat with my head down on the desk as the teachers taught, just reliving the weekend in my mind. I could not get it out of my head. In math class, Mr. Glenn's harsh voice startled me.

"Jackie, are you sleeping? Keep that head up and get to work."

I raised my head and looked at him with red eyes. I got up and walked out the door even as I heard him yell, "I'm calling security."

Thinking back to this day, I understand my mom reacting the way she did. I had been drinking and having sex since the age of fourteen. Her daughter was out of control. She wanted to save me. Recently, my mom and I talked about my wild teenage years.

"I am so glad you made it through that time in your life. I thank God every day for bringing me my girls," my mom told me. She is not the same mother of my teen years. The last vestiges of anger died with my father. I am thankful for my mom, for our healed relationship, and for her never giving up on me. My mom almost died during the Covid outbreaks. So, we keep a close eye on her now. She is eighty-three years old. All of her brothers and sisters are dead. All she has is us.

Education of a Teacher

My own experiences with teachers within the educational system were not always inspiring. In kindergarten, Mrs. Buell spanked me for going the wrong way on the tricycle path. My mom went to see Mrs. Buell and said, "No one hits my daughter. I am moving her out of your class." I was moved immediately to Mrs. Bird's class, whom I loved. I also learned not to trade classes with Juanita, my twin sister. We got caught. Juanita is not spelled with a W.

In third grade, I had a male teacher, Mr. Rover. He was tall and had a son named Elmo. Mr. Rover was athletic and often took us out for P.E. I will never forget the joy when he brought out a huge parachute for us to run under on the grass. It was my first time discovering the athleticism within me. I remember bolting in and out from under the huge, multi-colored parachute. Many years later, I recalled that same feeling when I began running marathons. Exercise and its power is part of my story. I even did my dissertation research on teachers' perceptions of student engagement after activity bursts in the classroom.

After I got sober, I was a marathon and triathlon participant for many years until Covid hit the world. Then, yoga and I found one another, and another love affair formed, uniting body and breath. Exercise is a must for me at the age of fifty-two. Five days a week, starting at 4 a.m., I go to the gym, meditate, and do yoga before my school day begins. This helps me lay the foundation for a positive day.

Students do not get enough activity in school. Many students, like me, need breaks and movement. Thank you, Mr. Rover, for inspiring me to give students plenty of brain breaks throughout the school day.

Remember the teacher from the last story? My high school math teacher, Mr. Wilson, was an authoritarian who would bark out the steps of a math problem only once. He expected students to understand the first time. I failed his algebra class and feared math teachers for years afterward. I felt stupid and incapable of learning math. Every day, when the class entered, Mr. Wilson would blow into his handkerchief and stuff it back into his cheap suit pocket. He would roam the room and order students to "Get to work and shut your traps." I've heard teachers my entire career say, "I teach the curriculum. I know my content better than most teachers, as I went to (insert Ivy League university here)." Learning doesn't come via osmosis for kids or young people.

A very different kind of teacher was Mr. Green, who was my math professor in community college. At first glance, it seemed like he would replicate my entire negative experience of white male teachers and math. Yet, when I struggled, he would ask me to stay after class and tutor me for hours during the quarter. Mr. Green welcomed questions, praised me when I worked slowly through the algebra problems, and eased my anxiety. I got an A in his class and ended up tutoring other students in his Math for Educators class. This is the power of a gifted teacher. They can help students master any subject.

My same friend, Melody, who was now teaching at an elementary school in the Inland Empire, allowed me to observe her class. After the observation, I spoke with Principal Thompson.

Principal Thompson and I talked for an hour about educational theory, high expectations, and behavior management.

"Melody is leaving for a new position. Would you like to teach here?"

"Are you offering me a job?"

"Yes." A new chapter of teaching began. Relationships matter. Looking back, I cannot fail to see how God was doing for me what I could not do for myself. This is not a religious book, but providence is a part of my story. I don't subscribe to any specific religion, although I was raised Catholic. Maybe it was my years of sobriety and reliance on a higher power I choose to call God that has helped me come to the belief that I am exactly where I am supposed to be. You know what they say about a turtle on a fencepost? If you see a turtle on a fencepost, you know she didn't get there by herself.

Elementary School Years

After working in a non-public setting with students with emotional disturbances, my elementary students were well behaved. They sat at their desks, listened when I taught, treated me with respect, and I did the same. We were a family. Teaching at a public elementary level school was peaches and cream compared to the non-public school. I taught in one of the two special day classes for students with mild to moderate disabilities. Students in the class had learning and sometimes behavioral issues.

Crystal was in my class that first year. She was a thin, pale girl with long, straight blond hair. She rarely smiled in class, at first. She would put her head on the desk and cry when asked to read aloud as she would stutter over even one-syllable words. I took her to the side and told her, "You need to try harder."

"I am trying, Ms. Mantz. I keep seeing the words all jumbled up." Her disability impacted her ability to blend multi-syllabic words. As a new teacher, I had no training in dyslexia. Dyslexia is a result of individual differences in areas of the brain that process language. Crystal would cry in our small reading groups, struggling to decode a first-grade text. What I realized through observation and assessment is that she could memorize sight words. She also had excellent comprehension of the material I read aloud to her. Every day before lunch, I spent twenty minutes reading aloud to the kids. I started with *Charlotte's Web*. Crystal raised her hand whenever I paused to ask a question about the story. She loved to listen to stories aloud, so I let her listen to the books on tape. She enjoyed drawing pictures of the plot, character, and theme while she listened. She began to feel successful when she saw her artwork and simple sentences on the walls of our classroom. Crystal smiled a lot more in class and even tried to read aloud in a small group. Reading never became her preferred task, but she did enjoy listening to stories and learned the elements of excellent storytelling. Teaching in elementary special education that first year helped me feel joy for small growth. Crystal and I developed a strong bond as younger children are more forgiving and resilient. They have not been beaten down by the education system, yet.

Disability is a complex issue. A student has so many strengths, yet the education system uses a deficit model. I disagree with the lens through which we see students with learning differences. The students I taught were smart in so many ways. They struggled in reading, writing, and math. Yet, with structured instruction, hands-on activities, and repetition, they learned. So, why did they have to be in special education?

In the year 2024, special education has made slow gains in the inclusion of students in special education into general education. Special education will be the final frontier of ending segregation in our society. Back in 2000, rates of Autism Spectrum Disorder (ASD) were much lower. This is due to under-identification and possibly other factors. Of the sixteen students, only one student had the qualifying disability ASD. Most of the students had the label of Learning Disability (LD), but I had other students with Other Health Impairments (OHI), which meant they typically had Attention Deficit Disorder (ADD) or Attention-Deficit/Hyperactivity Disorder (ADHD).

New teachers need the most training, but sometimes they get

the least support. During my first three years of teaching, I was on an emergency credential. No one except my principal and vice-principal observed me. There was no mentoring program. I worked on my preliminary credentials while I taught. During the summer, I did my student teaching in a middle school general education classroom so I could get my general education credential. I would not use this credential for twenty years. But when I needed it, I had it.

In contrast, new teachers who are clearing their credentials or those who get jobs as interns in my current district in the Coachella Valley have a teacher coach they meet with once a week for an hour. Recently, our district partnered with a university to form a resident teacher program. Resident teachers work with a master teacher in a classroom for one year. They attend classes in the summer before the school year begins and then take courses throughout the year. At the end of the school year, teachers receive their teaching credential and a master's degree in education. This newer model of teacher preparation programs allows resident teachers practical experience as they learn theories of teaching. I am honored to be teaching a course in the summer of 2024 to the second cohort of new resident teachers. The course is on inclusive practices in special education.

My fourth through sixth grade special day class classroom was my home for six years. It is where I learned the science and art of teaching. Learning how to get students to learn from your teaching is a science. The art of teaching is the performance aspect. I loved to ham it up with the class singing, dancing, doing voices, and bringing puppets to life before the students' wide eyes.

Our classrooms were well funded in those days. Principal Thompson allowed me a wish list, so I bought a huge rug of the United States, manipulatives (blocks and other objects that allow students to learn in a hands-on way), a treasure chest with prizes, and classic children's books on tape. I had a bookshelf full of paperback books for the kids and an overhead projector.

As a new teacher, I learned as much from the kids as they learned from me. It is important to learn what does and does not work. This is the science of teaching. All great teachers are researchers. For example, I struggled to teach phonics, but at that time, the curriculum was scripted in language arts so at first I just followed the script. Then, I gave it my own flavor and improvised like I was part of a comedy troupe, and that was when kids learned the most. It's called engagement, right? We sang songs for multiplication, acted out stories, painted our vocabulary words, and I leaned on Ms. Figueroa, my next-door neighbor and special education teacher, for help in doing science projects.

I learned that elementary kids were more sensitive than high school students, that structure and a schedule were foundational. Also, elementary kids responded well to hands-on learning, songs, games, and a positive reinforcement system that used a checking account to reward their good behavior. I still remember the joy at the end of the year of doing an auction with the kids. Some students had saved up all year to buy the board games or stuffed animals I found through donations. Teachers stay despite the long hours and low pay because learning can be magical. In teacher speak, it's called the Zone of Proximal Development, a theory of learning constructed by Lev

Vygotsky (1978). It is defined as the difference between what a learner can do without assistance and what a learner can do with support from a teacher or in collaboration with more academically advanced peers.

No one told me how physically demanding a job teaching in a classroom was. Kids were always sick, and as a result, I got sick more often. They would crowd around me, coughing and sneezing. Some students struggled with using the restroom and wiping themselves appropriately. I had to teach students how to use the restroom? Where was this in my non-existent teaching manual?

Wanna Buy a Watch?

Peter was a student with a charming smile, a sense of humor, and an intellectual disability. He struggled with learning but loved hands-on activities and sports. He also loved coming to school as he could always entertain himself and others. One morning, after the Pledge of Allegiance, Peter stood up and raised his hand.

"Wanna buy a watch, Ms. Mantz?" Peter asked, displaying a brown arm decorated with an assortment of watches: a gold watch, a Timex watch, and even a neon green Swatch watch. The class erupted in laughter, and I couldn't help but join in.

"No thanks, Peter. Where did you get all of those?"

"I have moves," he said, smiling, his brown curly hair a halo around his round caramel dimpled face. Inside Peter's tall, lanky frame and green eyes resided a budding comic.

"Can you count by fives with your fingers and tell me the answer, please, since you have such moves?" I asked, displaying my hands and counting, bringing my fingers down one by one.

"Thirty."

"Thank you, Peter. Will you sing the sixes song? Remember it goes like this: 'There was a farmer who had a dog and Bingo was his name oh, 6, 12, 18, 24, 30, 36, 42, 48, 54, and 60.'"

At 3:10 p.m., as I was helping my students onto the school bus, I watched Peter, with my mouth agape, run into the street and plop down prone in the middle, in front of an ambulance that was stopped at the light. I immediately ran over, but Ms.

Cervantes, the vice-principal, stopped me and said, "Let me handle this." Ms. Cervantes walked calmly over to Peter and said in a stern voice, "Get up now." Peter jumped up and walked with Ms. Cervantes to the office. I tried to talk to her about the incident, but she said that Peter pulled these stunts from time to time. I decided to call his mom after I got back to my room and could breathe.

"Hello, is this Peter's mom? This is Ms. Mantz. How are you? Yes, I saw what happened outside today. I am glad Peter is okay. What is going on with Peter? Today he had all these watches up his arm. Do you know where he got them?"

"Those were his dad's watches. He likes to wear them to remember him. Peter's dad passed away last year," she said. I listened as she continued. "He was shot, and Peter saw it all. He's still dealing with it. The last time Peter saw his dad alive was in an ambulance." I continued to listen, my hand gripping the phone.

"Thank you for telling me this. Is there anything you know I can do to help Peter? I know he likes to be funny, so I let him tell jokes in front of the class at the beginning of the day. Is there anything else?"

"Help him learn to read and teach him to stop peeing his pants. I'm tired of bringing him clothes to school." The next day, Peter peed in his pants again. His face crumbled when kids complained about the smell.

"Peter, please just go to the bathroom. You can just do the sign and go," I said as we spoke outside. Ginny, the paraeducator, monitored the class while the kids worked on their handwriting. They would do handwriting practice for an hour if I let them.

"I'm sorry, Ms. Mantz," Peter said. I had no answers. We created a schedule of bathroom breaks and walked kids to the bathroom every two hours. Nothing worked. Peter's mom brought extra clothes that we stored in a cupboard, but his walk of shame troubled me. The kids tried to call him names and make fun of him. I addressed this behavior immediately with discussions one-on-one with kids on kindness and empathy. Still, I knew something had to change.

One day, when we were leaving school, Peter walked up to me with his clothes in a bag.

"Ms. Mantz, I'm sorry. I'm so sorry." He then grabbed my arm and went down on his knees. "Please forgive me." I looked at Peter and sighed.

"Peter, the time for sorry is done. I'm not mad at you. Stop saying sorry, and let's work together to help you change!"

Peter stopped, cocked his head, and smiled. "Okay, can I tell you a joke now?"

I laughed as I didn't want to cry.

Teachers are not oracles but people just doing the best we have with what we have, just like Peter. Now, I would make sure to refer Peter for mental health counseling. His bathroom issues and incidents with the ambulance were a cry for help. Underneath the humor, Peter suffered. Peter and I had another talk one day when he and I were waiting for his mom to bring him some replacement clothing.

"Ms. Mantz, I want to drive an ambulance when I grow up. That way I can help people like my dad who died," he said.

"That's a lovely goal, Peter," I replied.

"Yeah, I'll get to use the sirens too," he whispered, and we laughed. The power of laughter within life is well known, but it is essential in the classroom too. In the book *Teaching Critical Thinking: Practical Wisdom*, bell hooks states that we "need humor as a mediating force" (hooks 12). Humor has been an omnipresent force in my classroom. I first realized the power of humor when I taught at the elementary school. Young children love to giggle. I loved teaching with puppets and using voices. I had a collection of strange, collectible trolls dressed in costumes that I let kids have on their desks to read with them. We would have joke time right before lunch. Laughter decreased the stress of learning and brought the class together. Many students in our elementary class had had negative experiences with reading, writing, and math, so I did my best to infuse laughter into the school day. I will clarify that laughter should never be at another person's expense. It is important to teach young children and teenagers the importance of kind, loving language in relation to themselves and others.

So laughter and love helped Peter become more comfortable and able to self-regulate his behavior, but this was not the end of the story, just the beginning. His mom and I had many more meetings that year, and we worked together to come up with a plan to help Peter manage his needs. By the end of fourth grade, Peter was able to manage his bathroom needs on his own. This success helped him become more self-confident with his peers, and he began to grow academically.

Peter was in my class from the fourth through sixth grade. By sixth grade, Peter was a role model to others while retaining his sense of humor and love of comedy. Yes, he still struggled in reading, but he learned to decode at the second-grade level. He could also state the main details of a story that was read aloud to him. In math, Peter thrived, eventually learning all his multiplication facts. This foundation allowed him to master division. He would struggle with word problems in math, but he loved to time himself doing a fluency math worksheet. When Peter walked across the stage in his suit at the sixth-grade promotion ceremony, I knew he was ready for middle school. His mom was there, and when we posed for pictures with Peter, I heard her whisper to him, "Your dad would be so proud. You look so much like him."

Remember that we do not teach books. We teach living, breathing humans with needs. People need to be loved and accepted. Students need to be nurtured. Then they can learn. We have to meet the kids' needs before we can teach them. Students learn best from people they know loves them and whom they love back. If you do not build relationships, they will not come on the learning journey with you. You might as well teach to the walls. Our words and actions would fall upon closed ears and minds. We need to open our hearts first.

But if you are teaching, remember you are human too. Make sure you use the restroom. There is such a thing as a teacher bladder or infrequent bladder syndrome. Many teachers do not take adequate bathroom breaks. This results in increased frequency, urgency, or leakage. I held my pee a lot during those first few years. Today, I go to the restroom every passing period. But, somedays, I still drink too much coffee and Diet Coke. This is when I call the office and ask Mo, our security guard, "Can you give me a restroom break please?"

Gap Two

Personally, I was still struggling with relationships. After a short romance, I married a man who had worked with me at the non-public school. That lasted two years and then we divorced shortly after I moved to the elementary school. He hurt me; I hurt him. I worked nights after teaching with my mom at Yangtze Restaurant to pay for the divorce. Then, I filed for bankruptcy. The last time I saw my ex-husband in person was twenty years ago. Recently, he popped up on Facebook, reading the children's book he wrote. I try to be happy for him. I do not know if he changed. I doubt it, even though I said I believe all people can change.

Now that you're aware I went through a divorce while teaching at the elementary school, here's another story about the challenges of having classroom pets. I thought having a class pet would be simple.

Hermit Crabs, Hamsters, and a Fish–Oh My!

My dream, when I was a bright little chubby Latina in the Gifted and Talented Education (GATE) program, was to have a teacher with a class pet. In my first year of teaching at the elementary school, I had two hermit crabs, SpongeBob and Patrick. They lived only a few months. We buried them in the playground under a tree. The next day, we saw the school bully with their shells around his neck, yuck. So, we had to find a new pet. A dog or cat was out of the question. I suggested a fish.

"Fish are boring," said the students. Then fate intervened. My friend Rosemary donated her hamster. She was a fawn-colored rodent who loved to run inside a plastic ball in her clear plastic cubicle. How much trouble could a little hamster be? I could take Clarice home on the weekends. During the week, she could provide students with untold joy.

Fifteen innocent students filed into the class with their hands behind their backs. My face broke out into a huge smile as the kids crowded around Clarice. "She is so cute, Ms. Mantz. I want to be a pet keeper! She is fat. Look, she is making a toilet paper blanket," said Jaime, a sixth-grade student. Clarice was loved by all. She roamed around the room in her clear plastic ball as long as everyone stayed seated and on task. But a few days later, Jaime was in the back of the class, getting a drink of water. All I heard was, "Oh my gosh, there are babies, under the toilet paper blanket!" Charlie Brown chaos ensued for the next three minutes. The kids crowded around the hamster cage in excitement. "Clarice is a mommy! I want a baby."

"I want a baby, Ms. Mantz, please!" All the students wanted a hamster baby more than a bike. I decided that the first few parents who consented could take the babies as soon as they were old enough to leave the toilet paper nest Clarice had created for her little family.

The next day, Jaime made a startling discovery. "Ms. Mantz, there are only nine babies now. Where did the other one go?" asked Jaime. When I moved some of the shavings around, I found the bloody remains. "Such is nature, children. Sometimes animals die," I told them, unaware that there was more carnage to come. Every morning, more of the baby hamsters were dead. I called a pet store, and they said that the classroom might be too loud. The hamster mother could not handle so much noise and attention. I chose not to tell my students this but just reminded them that they were lucky to be human children.

By this time, the joy of Clarice was gone. She was a murderer in their eyes. None of my students wanted to take her home. I could not stand to look at this seemingly harmless hamster who had robbed my young students of their innocence. On Friday, a student from the class next door knocked on my door. Angelo had thick Buddy Holly glasses and a mom who worked as a recess aide. "My mom said you want to get rid of Clarice. Can I have her? I want to take her home, and I'm going to change her name to Hannibal."

"You can have her," I said, quickly loading Clarice into his arms, cage and all, minus her babies who were all buried by a tree outside. He had brought his wagon with him.

"Salamat," Angelo said as he wheeled Clarice home. It was a relief to rid the class of Clarice's deathly energy. The next year, I bought the class a goldfish we named Sue. Sue lasted only a year, probably due to the small size of her bowl and overfeeding by the students who liked to see her eat. After these class pets, I had had enough. Plus, I was using up any extra energy to write a twenty-page Individual Education Plan (IEP) for students.

Teaching is a challenging job, but the paperwork side of special education is daunting. As a special education teacher, I was responsible for teaching and ensuring compliance by conducting annual IEPs, triennial IEPs, and amendment IEPs for students. Each document was approximately twenty pages long. Back in 2000, there were no IEP writing programs, so I wrote them by hand. Being left-handed, writing by hand was challenging. A few years into teaching, software was developed to assist with IEPs, which greatly helped. I enjoyed observing a student's growth and devising goals that were feasible for them to achieve within a year. However, trying to juggle two roles simultaneously was overwhelming.

We frequently held IEP meetings that consumed my three prep periods per week. When was I supposed to find time to write IEPs? I ended up writing them at night, on weekends, and during my lunch breaks. Additionally, I had to arrange all the meetings, and some students required multiple meetings per year. There was little training on writing an IEP in my district. I learned to craft effective IEPs through trial and error.

Every special education teacher has a caseload which can reach up to twenty-eight students. Every IEP necessitates a meeting with parents, all support providers, administration, and teachers in attendance. Additionally, every quarter or semester, we had to produce progress reports for each student, in addition to report cards. Feeling exhausted already? This is just a glimpse of the paperwork involved in the role of a special education teacher. Remember, we also need to teach.

Gap Three

I want to mortar these bricks into place, build a wall of apology. I started dating a woman after my divorce when I taught at the elementary school. Then, we got engaged. I was not ready to be married or "out" twenty years ago. I broke off our engagement, telling her, "Someday you will be loved." Oh, how I hurt her, with my callous words and actions. Don't—I won't—blame it on homophobia. Okay, maybe my own internalized hater. She's even worse than the teacher who said to me in the break room, "You shouldn't be a teacher if you are going to do that kind of thing." That kind of thing? Love is love. That's why I tell my truth today. Remember I'm unlearning shame. I'm fifty-two years old, still unlearning all I was taught by society, textbooks, media, my family, and me. I taught me to hate myself. But you know, if I can teach myself to hate, I can teach myself to love. This book isn't just for every student I taught; it's for me. It's for you. It's for us.

Clenched Fists on a Ferris Wheel

There are students one never forgets. They linger in one's heart and memories. Cooper was one of those kids. Cooper sat near my desk with his fists clenched. It was just another day in my classroom. The kids sat in a circle listening to me read aloud from *Tuck Everlasting*. Cooper's dark brown face was screwed up in a grimace, and he rocked back and forth on the chair. He had been sent home due to lice recently and came back with his head shaved.

"Cooper, do you want to come back to the circle?" I asked. "Leave me alone," Cooper yelled back, so I did. I read aloud:

The first week of August hangs at the very top of summer, the top of the live-long year, like the highest seat of a Ferris wheel when it pauses in its turning. The weeks that come before are only a climb from balmy spring, and those that follow a drop to the chill of autumn, but the first week of August is motionless and hot. It is curiously silent, too, with blank white dawns and glaring noons, and sunsets smeared with too much color (Babbitt 1).

Cooper's eyes darted back to the circle.

"Okay, class, let's talk about Ferris Wheels. Who has ever been on a Ferris wheel?" A few hands went up, including Cooper's.

"Ferris wheels scare me. They go up so high, but when I got down, I wanted to go again," Maria said, whipping her long, curly dark hair back and forth and smiling, showing off her dimples. Cooper raised his hand again when she finished talking. "I'm hungry, Ms. Mantz," he said. I displayed a colorful picture of a Ferris wheel, and Ms. Davis, the paraeducator, continued to lead the class in discussion. Cooper gripped a pencil in his grasp.

"Cooper, I have a sandwich in my bag. Do you like ham and cheese on Wonder Bread?"

"I don't want to take your lunch," Cooper said, shaking his head.

With a smile, I showed him I had two sandwiches. The rest of the kids were looking, so without a word, Ms. Davis passed out miniature bags of goldfish. "You can draw your Ferris wheels and have a snack," she told them. The kids drew Ferris wheels on paper as they munched on their goldfish, and then Ms. Davis wrote a sentence frame on the board for them to copy and fill in below their pictures: Ferris wheels are______.

Cooper had lunch at my desk. We didn't say anything. He finished his sandwich quickly.

"Are you ready to go draw your Ferris wheel?"

"I ain't never been on a Ferris wheel, Ms. Mantz."

"Can you draw one from the picture on the board? You're a good artist, Cooper." He turned to walk back to his desk. He stopped, though, and moved a bright orange piece of copier paper from the corner of the desk. On the desk, Cooper had scratched "FUC U" with his pencil.

"I did that, I'm sorry."

I was sorry he did not spell the word right. "Thanks, Cooper, for taking responsibility. Can we talk about this at lunch so we can figure out how you can make it right?"

"Yes, Ms. Mantz." At lunch that same day, Cooper came in and cleaned all the desks with a sponge and paper towels. The next day, he vacuumed. Every day that week, Cooper came and cleaned something. On Friday, I said, "We're all good. Next time, Cooper, just ask for a snack." He replied, "Yes, ma'am." This restoration was for him, not for me. I wanted him to forgive himself, as I already had.

Why didn't I call home or send Cooper to the principal's office? Every student's home life is different. I knew his mom was in the throes of a crack addiction. My principal taught me to try to handle issues in my own classroom before I involved him. This was a useful lesson, and it worked for me my entire teaching career. Cooper had ongoing issues with anger and fighting, and he struggled with reading. But, he knew I cared. I called Child Protective Services (CPS) a few times in my career as a teacher. Cooper frequently came to school in the same clothes. He was always hungry. Nothing changed for Cooper despite the numerous calls to CPS. On our last day before winter break, I gave all my students a small Christmas gift. Cooper also got a tote bag full of nonperishable food. I put goldfish, soups, and chocolate pudding cups. Cooper loved pudding cups, just like me.

Six years later, a few months before I left elementary to teach high school, a tall kid in jeans and a T-shirt came up to me as I walked out of the doors of the school office. He looked at me and smiled.

"Hey, Ms. Mantz, guess who?"

"Cooper, is that you? How are you?"

"I'm good, I just started at the high school, and I wanted to see my favorite teacher." We walked together and went into my classroom. I brought out a couple of cold waters from my fridge and some chips. As we snacked, Cooper told me how it was going.

"School sucks, but I'm gonna finish for my ma," he said. I walked Cooper out, and we hugged goodbye. I went to the high school graduation when Maria invited me, but Cooper was not in that graduating class.

I thought occasionally about Cooper for years, praying for his health and safety. I never heard from him again. I hope that he graduated high school and has all he needs to live a peaceful life. Maybe his kids now go to the elementary school I taught at. I hope he takes them on the Ferris wheel at the local carnival too.

Some people may see these stories as too saccharine for their tastes. I want to make it clear that I could not save students from their home lives or from the consequences of their behavior later in life. I do not know where Crystal, Peter, or Cooper are today, but they knew they were loved by me. I am sure of it. I was taught to love by a father and mother who were imperfect, so I loved imperfectly. However, I think I was my best self within the classroom as I knew the awesome responsibility I had been given. I am and always was proud to be a teacher.

But running a positive, well-organized classroom requires help. Some teachers like to pretend they can do it alone. Some years, I needed all the help I could get. Paraeducators or classroom aides are essential support in the special education classroom. I've worked with many paraeducators in my class throughout the years. Ginny Davis went on to become a teacher. She was "Ms. Organized" and kept me on track. When I first started teaching elementary school, the number of subjects overwhelmed me. Plus, I had to teach math, though I was better at teaching reading and writing. I was an organic teacher by nature, who loved teachable moments. A teachable moment is an event that provides an opportunity for learning about a particular aspect of life. Sometimes, I would let the kids distract me with their questions, and I would just tell stories about my life growing up with my two sisters.

"When I was your age, my sisters and I would ride our bikes and deliver newspapers. It was our first job. My twin and I had these little yellow bikes, but my little sister got a pink bike. Boy, were we mad." I would have continued on and on, but Ginny kindly said, "Umm excuse me, Ms. Mantz, but it's time for math now." When we got involved in our reading, writing, or art and lost track of time, she would sing, "Clean up, time to clean up..." Paraeducators play a pivotal role in the education system.

Another paraeducator I worked with during those years was Rita Jordan. Rita was phenomenal as she could quell nonsense with just a look and an "Umm, hmm." Her greatest gift was her smile. Kids beamed when she smiled at them. We had an annual talent show, and our kids wanted to participate. I always played a lot of music in class. The kids loved James Taylor's song, "You've Got a Friend." Rita took sign language classes. She suggested we teach the kids how to sign the song and sing along to it for the talent show. So we did. She taught the kids the signs for the song in the afternoons during art time. My student Ruby's mom, Michelle, was a nurse. She loved to donate supplies. During morning duty, I saw Michelle wave me over, already in her scrubs, her long black hair pulled back in a ponytail.

"I bought you all some shirts and fabric paints for your talent show coming up. Thanks for all you do," she said and drove off. Ms. Jordan did the shirts with them the day before. On the day of the show., the kids were all dressed in their bright yellow shirts with their handprints all over the back and "You've Got a Friend" painted in beautiful writing by our own Ms. Jordan.

As they sang and signed the song led by Ms. Jordan, Ms. Figeroa and I wiped tears from our eyes. There was a standing ovation. Although there were no trophies, we all knew who took first place.

My students' parents were always open to helping if they could. I never asked, as I understood some families were just trying to survive. But I never turned down an open offer to donate time or supplies. Many parents would often come in the morning or after school and push steaming plates of food into my hands. Maria's mom always brought me fresh buñuelos. Peter's mom brought me collard greens. I ate well and often as an elementary teacher.

My kids ate well too. I always had snacks for them. They liked goldfish, pretzels, granola bars, and chips (their favorite). I've been reading Pulitzer Prize winner Frank McCourt's lesser-known book, *Teacher Man*. Many people know his classic memoir, *Angela's Ashes*. Some know he was also a New York City high school teacher for thirty years. One recent morning, I couldn't stop laughing while reading about McCourt eating a student's sandwich on his first day as a teacher. I never took a student's lunch. In my family, we share food. My twin and I have been known to even share corn on the cob. One of my unwritten rules is I do not eat in front of kids unless I have a small snack for them too like goldfish or popcorn.

To pop into the future of my teaching career for but a moment. I still remember Adam, a student I taught in high school, who had a penchant for bags of Hot Fries. Adam knew I loved them too and would quietly put a small pile on my desk on a tissue or napkin. Adam now works at a local high-end grocery store. I see him from time to time, and we always quickly catch up.

"Hey, Ms. Mantz, how's life? You still teaching?" asked Adam.

"Yup, I'm working at the continuation school now. Love it. Can I get a half pound of macaroni salad?" I asked.

I let kids eat in class. If I can eat, they can eat. Now for teachers who do otherwise, good for them. But like Frank McCourt, my father was food deprived as a child. He always taught us to feed people. If you know Maslow's hierarchy of needs, you understand young people must have their basic needs met before they can learn.

A piece of advice I always give new teachers is to utilize all your human capital. Human capital includes your paraeducators, other classroom support staff, school staff such as custodians, parents, community members, and administration. At one of the middle schools today, I talked to Mr. Davon. Mr. Davon worked in the classroom with me as a paraprofessional years ago. He is now a special education teacher. He told me, "Dr. Mantz, I tell the paraprofessionals in our class that I am training them to be teachers. I got that from you." He is now pursuing a doctorate in education. Mr. Davon is a special education teacher, a wrestling coach, and a black male. We need teachers who look like our student population with doctorate degrees to show kids if we can do it, they can do it.

During my time teaching at the elementary school, the custodian Manuel Rodriguez and I became friends. He was a retired member of the military. He explained to the class the importance of a clean campus, the safety protocols he followed, and why it was important to "give a hoot and not pollute."

Luis, a student who had a hard time with school and staying in class, took to following Mr. Rodriguez around campus at lunch and at recess. He learned how to sweep, empty the trash, and even got to eat lunch with Mr. Rodriguez once a month when he stayed in class consistently. This was with administrative approval. I still remember how Mr. Rodriguez at the end of the school year came up to me and pressed a hundred-dollar bill into my hand.

"This is for yours and Martha's kids. Have a big party for them. They work hard. My son Manuel was in special education, and he had teachers like you and Martha." Until I left, Mr. Rogriguez stayed an integral part of our support system for the kids.

I suffered as a child with anger. Most of it was internalized when I was younger. As I grew older, I turned to books, food, and then alcohol for escape. I was awash in chaos and afraid. According to Don Miguel Ruiz in the article "The Track of Love or the Track of Fear?," "Anger is nothing but fear with a mask." Here's another story from my childhood so you may understand my story and seek to understand others.

Eye of the Beholder

Juanita, Annie, and I sat on the floor in front of the television and watched a Plastic Man cartoon, still in our pajamas on a peaceful Saturday morning. Daddy was making his famous peanut butter Mickey Mouse pancakes, eggs, and thick, crispy bacon. I walked behind Daddy and grabbed a piece of bacon. His bacon was epic, with just the right amount of crispy crunch. It was best right out of the pan, though it was liable to burn the top of your mouth.

"Jackie, stop, wait till I'm done. You're going to finish the bacon before anyone gets any." Daddy's voice was stern but playful.

"Please, let me just have one more piece, please," I pleaded, hoping to coax another strip from him. With a chuckle, Daddy relented. "Here, don't tell your sisters." He passed me one more piece, and I savored the salty goodness as I returned to my spot on the floor.

During the commercials, I got up again and walked away from the television toward the kitchen. I watched him pour the bacon grease onto another skillet. Any home cook knows bacon grease adds even more flavor to the pancakes and eggs. Daddy believed the older the grease, the better the taste. None of us ever got food poisoning. Even now, I have a vintage canister filled with bacon grease on my counter. Daddy's girth spoke of his passion for fattening food. He grinned and danced as he created his culinary masterpieces. Stains marked his once-white T-shirt, and his hair was askew. He would often say, "My greatest joy is making sure you girls are well fed. Why do you think I go to the grocery store so often?"

Just then, Mom walked in, yelling, "That damn car overheated again!" She threw the milk on the counter. Annie went to her room. Juanita sat frozen by the television. I was stuck in the kitchen, and there was no path around my mother. I felt the force of my mom's anger, and the bacon grease bloated my mouth, and I desperately wanted to throw up. I hated Mom for ruining the taste of bacon in my mouth and for putting that look on Daddy's face. He wasn't singing or dancing anymore. I did not say a word; I stood there and made an evil wish. I wished my Mom away to the cornfield. I whispered to myself, "Please go away." I knew television wasn't real. But I yearned for some power even as a little kid. In *The Twilight Zone* episode "It's a Good Life," Anthony has god-like mental powers and can wish people away to the cornfield. I wanted the mom who had taught me how to read and bowl and held my hand when I got bit by a dog to appear. This woman was an angry witch casting a sickly spell upon the day.

The tirade continued, and Juanita stepped in when called. She filled up a bucket with water and followed Mom outside. I went to the front door and watched from afar.

"Mom, I got the water. What are you doing?" Juanita asked. "Oh, you're going to cool down the car. Are we still going to see Grandpa today?" Juanita's calm demeanor contrasted sharply with Mom's anger, diffusing the tension in the room. I observed the scene unfold, my heart heavy with resentment. I kept looking back at Daddy, then outside. Daddy's shoulders slumped, but he continued cooking, his movements slow and deliberate.

"Girls, sit down and eat. Where's Annie?" he asked, attempting to regain a sense of normalcy amidst the chaos. Annie mysteriously appeared as if she were Plastic Man seeping into the cracks in times of difficulty. She was as calm and serene as a baby Buddha. Her long, dark black hair, pale skin, and pink ruffled pajamas made her look more like a doll than a four-year-old girl. I sat down and ate even though I was not hungry. The weight of food dulled my anger at the witch. It was quiet now, and Daddy struggled to fill in the time of waiting.

"Girls, when I was your age, all I got to eat was bread and grease. We used to just get a piece of bread with grease on top and some milk. That was our breakfast. I remember I used to dip my bread in the milk." He dunked his pancake in his coffee and ate it. Annie and I giggled.

"You're funny, Daddy," said Annie. Juanita walked in confidently. She sat down, and her skinny frame devoured a pancake, two pieces of bacon, and a greasy egg.

"Mom's fine now. She's going to cool down the car, and we can go to Carl's Jr.'s for lunch."

I had a mouth full of bacon and eggs, but my mind was drawn to lunch now. I began to plan my meal. I was going to get a Western Bacon Cheeseburger, French fries, and a Coca-Cola. Mom ran into the house, holding her face.

"I burned it!" she screamed. This was worse than the swear words, worse than rage.

"Help! The water burned my face! Help me, girls, John, help me. It hurts so bad. My face is burned." Mom cried out in pain. I was riveted by her red face. She ran to the sink and put ice on it. In *The Wizard of Oz*, Dorothy defeats the bad witch by throwing water on her. But my mom was no witch. I started crying. Daddy held Mom like a child and pressed ice to her face.

"Girls, go to your rooms and read or something," he said. I went to the restroom, stuck my finger down my throat, and threw up bacon, eggs, and pancakes in chunks. I felt better. This was not the first time or the last time I would throw up food when upset.

The next day, a Monday, I stayed home sick from school. Daddy came home on his lunch hour and made me one of his famous hamburgers. He cooked the hamburger patties on a skillet and put lots of mayonnaise on the Wonder Bread.

"Can you put extra pickles on it, Daddy?"

"Sure, I'm putting some raw onion on it. That should help your cold." He winked. Daddy knew I wasn't sick physically. He got two glasses out of the cupboard, added ice, and poured Diet Shasta Cola into them. We sat together on the couch in the living room. I felt warm in his presence and calm as we munched our lunch. We watched an episode of *The Twilight Zone* together, the one that begins with a woman's face wrapped in bandages.

He left after the pigs' faces were revealed in the episode. I marveled at the plot twist. Under the bandages, the character, Janet Tyler, looked like a movie star. She had blond hair, pale creamy skin, big dove eyes, and full lips. I wanted to look like her. But she was hideous according to this world's idea of beauty. At the end of the episode, the handsome character in a suit, Walter Smith, who is taking her to a village to be with her own kind, tells her, "Beauty is in the eye of the beholder... say it over and over to yourself."

"You're beautiful, and I love you," Daddy said as he walked out the door, and I went back to bed to cuddle with my cat Greye and read another Harlequin romance novel.

I talked to my mom about this incident. My parents had an old brown car; at the time, it was always overheating. My mom didn't have insurance, so she didn't go to the hospital.

"We didn't have any money, Jackie. Dad wasn't working. The bar was bankrupting us. We were losing our home. We had a lot going on and then I burned my face. I was always rushing around, trying to hold it together. I still have a little brown scar from it," my mom told me.

"Why do you think you were so frustrated back then, Mom?" I wanted to understand her emotions better.

"My life was falling apart, and your dad was gambling and drinking. I was working two jobs and tired all the time. I had three kids, remember that too. I had to wash clothes and cook dinner," she explained.

"Why didn't you leave him?" I probed further.

"I loved him, Jackie. Like you love Joe. I really cared for him. He helped me want to live after I lost David. He helped me through it. That's why. Life is hard."

Today, I see my mom's struggles and understand that her anger stemmed from overwhelming pressure and difficult circumstances. Last week, my mom fell. She broke her nose and gashed her face on her stove's glass front. But she did not break any bones. When I sat in the emergency room, holding her hand while the doctor stitched her up, I knew that angry child I used to be was healed. All I have is love and admiration for my mom. My family is beautiful and complex, like many.

Fang Face

I am like a train without steam after Boomers Amusements
before smiling and free like a bird in my favorite orange tank top
and corduroy pants, hatching a plan to capture my heart's desire
a boy, a handsome cruel boy, with blue eyes like my daddy
who loved me. So why shouldn't he?

Now a caged smile, covered by hands over mouth
I want to throw up, get rid of yellow chunks of memories
his words, "I would NEVER date Fang Face."
The technicolor night turned charcoal gray.

Daddy drives up in his red Chevy Beretta
in his too-tight shirt, John belt buckle, and sneakers
loved those sneakers, "Hey my beauty, what's wrong?"
I sob in his arms, all is well, Daddy thinks I'm beautiful.

Glittering Promise

Thinking back to my years spent teaching elementary school, I see now how I mothered my students. Sometimes, as a teacher, you have to do what is best for the kids. This can take the form of advocating for them to move out of the special education setting. I remember Maria.

"Please don't make me go. I love you and Ms. Figueroa," Maria pleaded, her long brown curly hair shaking as she sobbed.

"Maria, we love you too," said Ms. Figueroa, her former special education teacher from first through third grade. Maria spent all her early elementary years as a budding English learner in special education classes. Martha sat with Maria and me in my classroom. We spoke to Maria about our plan to move her into a general education class in January. Maria was by far the highest achieving student in the class, reading at grade level in both Spanish and English and mastering long division and fractions. She did not have learning disabilities but was placed in special education due to her diagnosis of mild cerebral palsy. Maria had spent kindergarten in a moderate to severe classroom because of the braces on her legs. Let me explain further, I want you to understand how this changed her trajectory.

Moderate to severe classrooms typically have students who are non-verbal, severely physically disabled, and severely delayed cognitively. These classrooms even have a different curriculum and focus on functional life skills. This was not the appropriate placement for Maria so she was then moved to the mild to moderate setting. Today, she would never have been placed in a special education class. Ms. Figueroa saw her potential and taught her to read and do math until she was at grade level. By fourth grade, Maria moved to my class, and at her IEP meeting, we decided to mainstream her into the fourth-grade dual immersion class taught by our best friend, Mrs. Betancourt.

We moved Maria in January as agreed upon. The next time Mrs. Betancourt and I spoke, she said, "All Maria does is cry all day in class. She's a weepy cherub. It's heartbreaking."

"We have to keep her there. Let's have lunch with her on Fridays, if she can stop crying. Why am I crying? That's my little girl, but I'll be damned if she stays in special ed due to her love for us," said Ms. Figueroa.

Two weeks later, on a Friday, we sat in my classroom, having lunch with Maria. We ate the beans and rice burritos Ms. Figueroa had made for us while Maria shared her experiences in the general education setting.

"Mrs. Betancourt is teaching us opera. We're singing a song from *Les Misérables*, and she's teaching me how to crochet. There's some really smart kids there. I have to work hard."

"Just always do your best, honey. We're proud of you," said Ms. Figueroa.

We kept up the lunches until the end of the year. Maria always showed up at the door on Fridays. By the next year, Maria was comfortable in her new general education classroom setting, but every so often, she would appear like a glittering fairy after school. She helped us clean and organize our rooms. She eventually moved to middle school, and I left the district to teach at a high school in the Coachella Valley.

In 2014, I was driving home from teaching at the high school when my phone rang.

"Jackie, guess who is graduating and invited us to attend? A few of our kids are graduating. Maria, Sean, Stacey, Mario, and Rhonda. Come with me to the graduation," said Martha.

"How about Robin?" I asked.

"No Robin. I have no idea where he landed," she said.

"Wow, I'll be there," I said. Still, my heart ached for our missing Robin. We sat through the long ceremony and cheered as our students' names were read. As they walked across the outdoor stage, our tears fell freely. We managed to find Maria, looking grown up in her cap and gown, her brown cascade of curls flowing down her shoulders. Her smile, that same dimpled smile, grew huge as she tottered toward us in sparkling pink high heels.

"Ms. Figueroa, Ms. Mantz, Ms. Betancourt! You came." Her parents stood smiling while Maria hugged us all and took pictures with us. Attending students' graduations and staying in contact with families is a tradition I continue to this day. I consider any student I taught family.

"We're meeting at Olive Garden tomorrow with Rhonda and Kathy at 11 a.m. so we'll see you soon," I said. We hugged goodbye, and I watched Maria walk with her parents to their car, her small figure leading the way. I stay in contact with Maria. She is in her late twenties now, currently in remission from cancer. We talked of her challenges brought on by the weight gain from steroids and kidney issues. Martha and I took her out to lunch again recently. Maria ran out in that loping stiff-legged run I knew from so many years ago, still bringing the butterflies with her smile.

Here's a poem for one particular former student, now an adult, though his whereabouts elude me. Despite my efforts, I've yet to find him. I pray someone recognizes this individual from the poem. We remember you, always.

Circles Over Circles

Two hundred pounds
rich coffee skin
Darth Vadar voice
six years old swaying
sings along to a song
cerebral palsy's gift
gait of a walking oak tree.

Sixth graders move to the side when
Robin walks by.

XL polo, size 40 Dickies
size 12 steel toe boots
runs in circles over circles
on the playground
obedient in class but mutters,
"Ummmm math nooooo.
God just baptized me Ms. Figlolo,
do Christians have to do math?"

Graduation day
elementary style
Robin in a suit, SeaWorld tie
Nana prays.

Ms. Fig hands
Robin a certificate
angels embossed in gold.

Nana shakes her head
this is the end of the innocence era.

Middle school
living with his evil mama
no image to convey the evil she do.

Scan the seats
where could Robin be?
Ms. Fig
holds hand
tells tale
thick throat
no hope.
Nana told me something
prepare.
Robin calls Nana on his
high school teacher's phone.

"Nana, I don't know what to do, Mama's not you."
No more calls, Mama put a stop to that
one more call to this story
so far.
Homeless with no shoes in San Berdo
running in circles over circles in a park

cuff his three hundred six feet
seventeen-year-old frame
police car riddles of shame
passerby remembers a child
with the gait of a tree and dimples deep.

"Is it you, Robin? Do you recognize me?"
Furrowed brow, a bowed head, wishing even more
God would help him, strike him dead.

"Yes, ma'am, I do,"
almost eighteen.
Will Robin make it home?
Don't know, don't know.

Moving On

During the six years I taught at the elementary level, I developed close relationships with students, parents, teachers, and administrators. Martha Figueroa and Linda Betancourt are still my close friends. Both are still teachers in the district I worked at, but both have moved schools. Martha left the special education classroom where she taught for over twenty years to work as a long-term substitute in the district, aiming to decrease her workload. Linda transferred to a different school. She needed a change. Both are content now in their new positions. Teacher burnout is a real issue, as evidenced by the unprecedented teaching shortage, especially in special education.

Back in 2002, I frequently conducted home visits with parents and kids. Many nights, I tutored kids in their homes if requested, bringing them workbooks from school. Parents supported me by volunteering in my class, feeding me despite my slight protests that I had brought my lunch (I miss those homemade greens, tamales, and pozole), and by doing their part in working with their kids on their homework, which consisted of multiplication songs, reading logs, and simple writing prompts. The students were so willing. They loved our classroom and worked hard on whatever assignments I gave them. By the end of the year, almost all the kids had mastered their multiplication facts, learned fractions, decimals, and percentages, and had become writers who could, with support, compose multiple sentences to multiple paragraphs, depending on their grade levels and abilities.

After six beautiful years of teaching at the elementary school, I moved to the Coachella Valley. For one year, I commuted, but gas prices skyrocketed, and my favorite principal, Mr. Thompson, retired. I remember when he did my second-year evaluation. I felt honored and seen.

"Before we start, Jackie, I just want to tell you that it brings tears to my eyes when I see you with your kids in the classroom. It's obvious they know how much you care. Keep doing what you're doing. You could work on bringing your voice down an octave sometimes," Mr. Thompson said. A supportive leader, he started with the positive, making me feel valued, and then discussed areas of growth. This is what we need more of in administration. Teachers need to feel valued and appreciated. Many do not right now, especially after the Covid years. Enrollment in teacher preparation programs is down due to the perception that teaching is a low-paying, stressful, disrespected profession. It can be, but there are wonderful schools and teams doing important work. As a teacher, I believe we have the right to move schools or even districts if one does not feel valued and supported. We can do beautiful work anywhere.

After Mr. Thompson left, the school was never the same. His positive mentality combined with his high standards had brought out the best in us. Mrs. Moreno was okay. But, she never told us what we did right. She only focused on the negative. I remember the one time I was late due to getting a flat tire in the rain. As I ran to get my kids, she looked at me and shook her head.

"You need to be on time, Ms. Mantz," she said. I just nodded. I was focused on picking up my students, but that was the moment I knew I was not seen. If she knew me, she would have known I was only late two times in six years, both for issues outside my control such as a flat tire. Due to the long hours, I knew I had to change schools as the commute was an hour each way. That time could be spent writing IEPs while watching *Top Chef* at home. I loved watching cooking shows even though I did not enjoy cooking. Nothing has changed there. Recently, I paid to take an Indian cooking class. Alas, I was the only one that just watched. After the class was done, I went to get takeout Indian cuisine. It is okay not to be good at everything. But, I am great at eating.

I started applying for teaching jobs in the Coachella Valley. I was offered a job teaching theater to students with disabilities. I didn't take it because I had interviewed with Wilson Worth for a high school special education teacher position and we clicked. Wilson had an easy smile and a warmth that radiated to his eyes. We just talked about life. At the end of our chat, he said, "So, I think you would be a great fit. You'll be teaching English, and Roma, the department head, will be an excellent support for you." It took me some time to get used to high school. Elementary students love their teachers without reservation. Building relationships is tougher with older students. They have more negative experiences centered around school. But those years in elementary school trained me well. Any classroom I teach in always has lots of bright colors, students' starred work posted on the walls, and a cupboard full of birthday cards and snacks.

Gap Four

I said you would never be in my book. Your actions inflicted deep wounds and my body remembers. Yet, our relationship paved the path for my future, albeit through a landscape of bruised spirit and flesh. We were together only two years, but I'll never forget what it felt like—a prison of fists. I used to be ashamed of my past and wanted to shut the door on it. But I'm unlearning shame. I ended it, though not without seeking support from my therapist, whose hand I needed to grasp as I uttered the words, "We are over." That was the turning point for my new sober life. I was comforted by my gray tabby cat Henry and the strength of the sober fellowship. I lost my home and many drinking buddies. Yet, amid the wreckage, I discovered the gifts of sobriety. So, thank you. Today, I am sober, and I have a life beyond my imagination. I forgive you. I forgive myself.

Why You Will Not Be in My Novel

Never will you appear in any form
anywhere in my novel.
Wiped from all memory banks
that night you bruised my ribs
with your fifteen kicks to my gut
little round bug in a ball
drunk and sober suddenly.

I will never ever write about you
or about that rage
a crimson film upon an eye.

Drunk on the poetry of alcohol and drugs
not drunk enough
remember the fear one day maybe
of a scar across my face
jagged pink line from a knife
from that Caligula pinkie ring of yours.

Let me remind you again,
you will never be in my novel.
I deny you.

I deny I would crawl in bed with you

like a child and spoon your back
push me away at first, would you
but finally give in with a guttural groan
rage would seep into the covers
warm us to sleep.

Underneath the Christmas tree
love finally died.

Presents thrown against the wall
and sober ninety days
torn out of my story right then.

Hit, kick, but do not abuse
Christmas, sacred is Santa Claus.

Never will I write how in a warm room of wood
holding my therapist's pale hand shivering
I said, "WE are over."

I will never relate how I cried
begged for you back upon your doorstep
slammed that yellow door in my face, you did.

Providence, you didn't want me back
right then, if you had opened the door
I'd still be lying, still, underneath rage.

I never thought I would be one of those women who would tolerate another person's physical abuse. It is not surprising, though, when you look at my childhood, that I was drawn to someone like her. I left her and never looked back. We had a condominium we had purchased together. I let it go into foreclosure. I remember thinking, Let it burn. My safety was more important than my credit score. Letting go of alcohol and *her* saved my life. Thank you, Lee (my therapist), for putting me on the road to recovery. You are remembered. You are not gone but just in a different form. In *Eulogy from a Physicist*, Aaron Freeman writes, "According to the law of the conservation of energy, not a bit of you is gone; you're just less orderly. Amen."

I think of Lee, my former therapist often. She was one of my greatest teachers. I wish you could have met her. She was stylish, but it was not just her silver spiky hair, dimples, or turquoise cowboy boots she wore that made her beautiful. She shone bright and lit up the room with her kindness and love. Her heart was an expansive universe. She helped me so much in the two years I worked with her before she passed on from cancer. She is one of my inspirations. The work we do with people matters. So, I breathe in and out the memory of Lee's wide smile and bright blue eyes into the classroom every year. Her love and acceptance of me during those dark, predawn years sustains me to this day. It was with Lee that I first began to write and heal. I wrote a letter to my mom in therapy that became a story titled "The Three Little Girls." Here is that story.

The Three Little Girls

A Sea of Brassy Day

There was a chlorinated sea once upon a time. A turquoise pool infused with slants of golden sunlight. The strokes of a little girl's browned flesh flapped against the water, lap after lap; a foamy background to the day. Her curly head moved to the left to breathe, to the right to breathe, and to the left again, like some nursery rhyme yet unwritten. Another little girl, almost a mirror replica of the first one except a little chubbier, lay buried in bubbles, battling in the Jacuzzi against dragons of steam. The little girl's toes sworded through the water as she held onto the edge of the pool floating on her back. The third little girl, the youngest, floated across that same water, making animals from clouds in a bubble above her head. Her long dark hair fanned out, an ode to Ophelia in her watery grave.

Their father, dear father, sizzled thick steaks on the grill, a cigarette in one hand, a spatula in the other, smoke filling the air. The fluorescent yellow potato salad and rolls sat quietly on the scarred picnic table, paper plates and the plastic tub of margarine keeping them company. The three little girls, for some reason, at the same moment, all took a deep breath and inhaled Kool menthol cigarettes mixed with charred flesh, a deeply satisfying dysfunctional potion.

Just then, their mother, dear mother, suddenly appeared in a red Chinese smock soiled with bits of greasy foo young and shrimp. Her eyes tabulated magically, with one look, the empty Budweiser cans. The mother frowned, then her eyes moved to the three little girls. Ordering them out of their sea of fun; to lie one after the other on faded, blue-and-white-striped bath towels; lying, drying, baking. Three little girls with waiting tummies growling for ribeye steaks and mustardy onion-infested potato salad that even now they taste and savor.

Once upon a time, this azul rectangular sea would hold the middle girl, the chubby twin, during the day and soothe her at night. Just knowing it lay outside her window gave the little girl, all the three little girls most likely, courage to face the dawning night. This simple body of water gave the girls the strength to survive the nights of shadows making puppet monsters on the ceiling and closet door, nights reeking of rising words in a Holly Hobbie oven of hate.

The three little girls never knew when their slumber would be transformed into dense forests of fear, when their father, dear father, would wander away from home into bars. Then, only then, would those three little girls be thrown into a nightmare of hiding on the roof or running underneath tears of stars. Sometimes, more than once, they would flee to the park, but a block away... Yet this land could not be the same as the one they lived in during the day; it could not be. They were somewhere else, a nightmare never-never land. The girls would stay in the pool in the glittering day as long as they could. Under the covers in the darkening night, they would try to do the same; trying to remember the pool was out there. Trying to remember that tomorrow, no matter what happened, they would all be there in the land of the turquoise sea, in the sun, alive and well.

Dawning Night

John Wayne's last film, *The Shootist*, was on television. The three little girls played Monopoly in the living room as their dear father watched television, smoking cigarette after cigarette, while "The Duke" played a dying man with cancer. If the three little girls could time-travel, they would see their father ironically playing that same story out in thirty years, wheezing out his last breath, the dark magician of death waving the wand of pancreatic cancer to seal their father's fate, two months after diagnosis. Maybe, if the wife had access to this crystal ball, she would have been kinder, more loving, and less sharp with words to her dear husband. Maybe if the mother could have gazed back into that crystal ball, she might have seen the damage she would cause the three little girls with her fits of chaotic rage. "Maybe" is a hideous word, ugly in its hope. There were no maybes as the night dawned dark and heavy with tension curtaining the house with every throw of the dice. The twins fought over a move in the game. The older twin cheated, the younger twin threw the board. The youngest sat there calmly as the two bickered, made up, and the game resumed. It was Saturday night and cleaning time for their dear mother. She would wash clothes, pick up the mess left by cyclones of childhood, and cuss the entire time. The three little girls paid it no mind; they knew danger, but it had not yet appeared. The father's show ended. Now it was night. Darkness settled over the land as did the flight in the father's soul.

"I'll be right back, girls," the father slurred. "I need cigarettes and more Budweiser. I'll bring you each back a present. I shall get you a PayDay, you a Big Hunk and you a Twix." He patted each girl's head as he walked slowly out the door.

"Daddy, hurry home okay," said the youngest. The father walked out into the night. The night was filled with plenty of maybes. *Maybe I'll just stop for one drink at the Palomino, one game of pool.* The mother heard the blue Ford pickup truck's engine as she moved the clothes into the dryer. She walked into the house with a plastic basket filled with clothes.

"Stop playing that game. Help me fold these clothes," she ordered. The girls silently began folding clothes, their sibling bickering done. They were one now. A climate of fear pervaded the house.

"Where did your dad go?" the mother asked. She was already different; the metamorphosis had begun.

"He went to go get beer and cigarettes," the eldest answered. "And he will be right back, he said so." There was no answer from the mom. The minutes ticked by, each longer than the last. Five minutes turned into ten minutes, ten minutes to eleven, to twelve, to thirty. The Monopoly game was put away as were the clothes. The three girls took their baths. Still, the father did not reappear. Thirty minutes became an hour. The hand of the clock shoved and pushed the mom's rage higher, now cuss words were dangerous blows. They fled from them, from the TV, into the younger twin's room as it was the furthest away from their once-dear mother who had changed into the darkest of witches. One whose wild curly hair and words made them cringe. They sat in the middle girl's room and looked at the pool, reflecting on the day.

"We had so much fun today. We should go to sleep," the eldest girl said. The words made sense logically, but words of logic did not rule this dark land.

“I want to look at the pool,” said the youngest. "I don't want to go to sleep. We might have to get up.” They sat on the bed quietly, the door closed against the spells of rage and the curses against them and their dear father... Then, the roar of the witch’s car. How long did they have? How many minutes would it take the witch to drive from their home to the bar and back? What if he was at a different bar? How long until the next bar? Experts, they were grabbing blankets, pillows, and jackets. Out into the night they went, hoping no one would see their shame. What fairytale law had they broken to take away their kingdom and transport them to this one? Their footsteps were almost silent. They knew the way to the park. The park was their night fortress. The park was their mother now that the witch had taken over their dear mother’s form.

They made it in five minutes and laid inside the stinky yellow playground equipment they had named the Stinky Cheese King. The twins had Wonder Woman pajamas on. They loved the Justice League. The youngest girl’s long, Snow White nightgown shone in the moonlight. They slept for a long time. They were awakened by the calls of their mother.

“Not yet, he’s not home yet. I can tell by the sound of her voice,” whispered the youngest. The three little girls fell back to sleep for what seemed like hours, the longest of nights. The middle girl, the chubby twin, dreamt of the sea outside her window. In her dream, she and her sisters swam in slants of golden sunlight surrounded by the azul waves created by the strokes of their arms in unison, stroke after stroke.

The Darkest Night Fled Suddenly As Did the Witch

"Girls, come home. Girls, come home. Girls, come home," called a voice. The dear mother returned with the retrieval of the drunken father found finally in the bar of the Palomino.

"Come get him. He was fast asleep on the toilet, good thing I cleaned the restrooms before locking up." The owner had called the house at 2 a.m., just when the witch was throwing out all of the father's clothes onto the front lawn.

"Girls, come home. Girls, come home..." No more words best left to the devil. The three little girls were no longer hated. They were loved, and even though it was night, they could once again feel the sun's rays upon them. They came willingly into the car. They walked like puppets, strings pulled by the mother's fingers, into the house where on the table lay a PayDay, a Big Hunk, and a Twix.

This was the first piece of writing I published with the Inlandia literary journal in 2011. May anyone who is struggling with addiction, mental health issues, or letting go of anything that does not serve them, find support. I know it gets better. I'm living proof. But you have to do the work.

High School Years

> "I always say that the young people are the future of the world, and if we start with them first, if we educate and develop a sense of tolerance among them, our future, the future of this world, will be in good hands for generations to come."
>
> —Erin Gruwell, *The Freedom Writers Diary*

Like everything beautiful in life that discovered me, I was prepared first through experience to see differences in others as a part of life. At the age of sixteen, I worked at a restaurant in Pomona, The Olympic Flame. It was my first waitressing job, and I worked with my mom. Notice, I use the word "waitress." That was the language of the time. I dislike the term "food server" as it sounds like servitude to me. A waitress had spunk. She was a working-class cultural icon. She was me. My mom always told me at work, "Make sure you treat everyone like they matter. Use your smile. You will make better tips if people like you." I use this dimpled curly smile now to greet kids at the door. "Good morning, lovely souls," I say as they enter the classroom.

At The Olympic Flame, I made a friend named Michael. Michael's dad owned the restaurant. Michael Jr. worked the cash register. He was smart, funny, and had Down's syndrome. Michael was twenty but acted like a teenager.

"Jackie, clean that table, dude. I need to seat it," Michael said. He was somewhat of a nag. At The Olympic Flame, the waitresses bussed all their tables. We didn't need a busboy. This way we had no one to tip out but Michael who got a few bucks from each waitress. Michael and I joked and giggled a lot when we were slow. Michael never shorted the till. He would count out change carefully as the owner, his dad Michael, always told him sternly, "Be careful and count all the change back. Check all the big bills for counterfeit." What I appreciated the most was Michael was not hidden. His mom and dad did not feel sorry for him. They expected him to work hard, just like them.

In high school, I took a remedial typing class that was run by Mrs. Garrett. There were some students with special needs in this class, and they became my friends.

"Jackie, you're really good at typing. Sit with these kids and help them. I'll give you extra credit," said Mrs. Garrett. I shook my long, platinum bangs out of my face and started working with them. I stopped my own typing practice and walked behind the students, observing them. I showed students where to put their hands on the keys. One kid had a helmet on and screamed when I touched his hands.

"Be careful with him, he bites," said Bernie, another student. Bernie struggled in typing due to his motor skills, but he kept at it. Mrs. Garrett passed out Hershey's Kisses to kids who kept practicing. I appreciated the candy and loved her positive spirit.

"Don't mistake my kindness for weakness, kids," she would say when kids tested her boundaries. She graded us on how we improved our baseline score on the pre-assessment typing test. She lived a growth mindset, accepting all students into her class. This was not the norm during the 1980s as segregation of students with disabilities was rampant. During lunch when I saw Bernie, he waved at me. I waved back.

"Bernie's a cool dude. He's funny as hell," I said to my friends. My crew had the gothic rock look going on as we were fans of The Cure, The Smiths, and Depeche Mode. I passed Mrs. Garrett's class and graduated high school. In community college, I had a friend, Laura, who had a learning disability and Tourette's syndrome, which made going on double dates interesting. Laura's perseverance in class inspired me. She studied for hours for quizzes. I did not study much. Laura and I read together sometimes, and I learned to wait as she sounded out the multisyllabic words.

So, I suppose, it may have been destiny that all these seemingly random experiences prepared me for the path of a special educator. My greatest strength was treating my kids like any other kids, accepting them, and seeing them as smart and capable. My goofy sense of humor was a bonus. But an excellent work ethic was needed as a special education teacher. The paperwork was a job in itself.

At the high school in the Coachella Valley, I taught ninth- through twelfth-grade English for students with disabilities. The students varied in their ability to read and write. At my former district, Erin Gruwell, the author of *The Freedom Writers*, spoke to us regarding her experiences and her path with her students. I remember telling Mr. Thompson, the principal of the elementary school where I worked for six years, "I want to have my kids write books like *The Freedom Writers.*"

"I will support you in anything you do with your kids," he said. I had planned on doing the book project with my elementary kiddos, but Mr. Thompson left and then I did. But, the seed had been planted. I decided now was the perfect time.

"So, I have an idea. How many of you have seen *The Freedom Writers* movie?" Most of my students raised their hands. I then passed out a photocopied excerpt of the first chapter of the book. Only a few students groaned.

"Wait, so stick with me. What do you think of reading a chapter from the book and then watching the same section of the movie?" They nodded so I continued. "We can then write our books using these prompts from the teaching companion." Thus began a five-year journey of working with students on their writings.

It was maddening trying to help fifty students edit and revise their writings using ancient word processors. Teaching writing requires a strong spirit, work ethic, and an ability to accept controlled chaos. At first, I thought we would only just write and put the stories on the walls of our classroom.

"We are going to create books too, right, Ms. Mantz? I bet we can get some blank books and tape our writing in them. We could even design the covers and draw pictures to go with each story," Alora said.

"Sure, we can do that," I said with a smile and a wink. Inside I gulped.

"Can we have a party at the end?" Alora asked. "Ms. Mantz, my grandma will make the pancit you love. Then we could read stories from our books."

I just had to find a way to make it happen. So I wrote a grant asking for five hundred dollars and bought blank hardcover books from Bare Books at $7 each. I wish there was all the digital support we have today, but there was something so organic about watching the books take shape. We (I wrote my book which I still have sitting on my bookshelf as I write these words) started with an introduction, then wrote poems, essays, short stories, and even songs based upon the books we read throughout the year.

Some students who had never written detailed stories and poems before began to write. I remember Adam sitting with the paraprofessional, Mr. Robertson, and working on his writing. Adam spoke and Mr. Robertson wrote down his words. There was no such thing as speech-to-text back then that was affordable or easily accessible. Every student had their own book. Many managed to write ninety pages in a school year with a book cover, table of contents, and illustrations. Others filled in fifty pages. Some only filled up twenty of the pages. Each student created a book of their own.

Some students' work was exceptionally well written. It is a myth that all students in special education are academically deficient. In my experience, students with high-functioning autism sometimes have high levels of writing if it is a preferred task or topic. I allowed these students to sometimes diverge from the writing topics with jaw-dropping results. One student wrote a series of zombie stories that horrified and enthralled me.

Students with the label of emotional disability could perform at high academic levels but struggled with school due to mental health. Alora wrote poetry laden with beautiful imagery inspired by her experiences in the Philippines. Spirit Cloud wrote pee-your-pants funny stories that demonstrated his wacky view of life and lots of love poems. He was always crushing on girls in the class.

I remember that first week with the kids. Spirit Cloud weighed about three hundred pounds, had a mop of curly hair, green eyes, and a booming voice. "Can I read first?" he yelled to the room of six kids, me, and Mr. Robertson. "Sure," I said. "Can you bring it down a bit, Spirit Cloud?"

"I'm not bringing it down, I'm bringing it up," he roared. Then, he jumped up on the table, clutching the pages of the first chapter of *The Freedom Writers Diary* in hand. "'Dear Diary, tomorrow morning, my journey as an English teacher officially begins.' Ms. Mantz, this sounds like you," Spirit Cloud said as he jumped down from the table and sat down.

"Well, Spirit Cloud, I am not a new teacher. This is my ninth year. I've taught at a non-public school, an elementary school, and now here at the high school," I said.

"Now you're with the crazy kids, the retards, and me," said Spirit Cloud.

Mr. Robertson cleared his throat. "Spirit Cloud, dude, don't speak like that about yourself or others. We're all here to learn and all of us can learn." Spirit Cloud filled up the entire ninety pages with his stories and poetry. He was quite the romantic.

Spirit Cloud went on to work at Walmart after graduation. For years, I would see him when I went shopping for food for my classroom. One morning before Christmas break a few years after he graduated, I saw Spirit Cloud at Walmart in his bright yellow vest and reindeer ears. He told me, "My mom has to work on Christmas. I'm staying home alone and going to make myself a filet mignon dinner."

"You can come to our house on Christmas day, Spirit Cloud," I replied.

"Awesome, I'll bring my bomb potato soup and the steak," he replied and hugged me.

That Christmas, my family and I welcomed Spirit Cloud to our Christmas dinner. His baked potato soup and bacon-wrapped filet mignon were the stars of our meal. But the highlight was Spirit Cloud's laughter and joy filling the room. My twin sister, Juanita, remembers him still. She asked me the other day, "How is your former student Spirit Cloud?"

"He got married then divorced. I know he moved to Las Vegas. I hope he is doing well," I replied. I then looked up his Facebook profile. Spirit Cloud has a lot more tattoos than when I last saw him. He also posts a lot of pictures of his culinary masterpieces. I messaged him, "Spirit Cloud, I haven't heard from you in a while. I will always appreciate the humor you brought into my life. Be well."

Every student in my five classes chose one piece of writing to share at the end of the year at our book reading. Parents, administrators, fellow teachers, and community members sat in my room and listened to Room 228's students tell their stories. Mack, one of our students who was a "Brony" (a boy who loves My Little Pony), was the master of ceremonies. He had black, spiky hair, wore a tuxedo blazer, and a top hat. To complete his look, he wore a My Little Pony T-shirt underneath the blazer. "Greetings, welcome to our grand galloping gala. Our first reader of the night is Spirit Cloud, reading a love poem," Mack said in a booming voice. Some years I managed to find enough sponsors to serve pizza, cookies, and Starbucks coffee for dessert. I ALWAYS bought a cake from Costco that had the words, "Congratulations, Writers of Room 228."

Mack graduated high school, went to Long Beach City College, got a job, and still keeps in touch. He wrote me a Facebook message in 2022:

"Hi Ms. Mantz, it's Teacher Appreciation Day, and I would like to say thank you very much for giving me such an educational opportunity in high school. Your passion for teaching others was clear to me when I saw you teach me and the other students the wonders of what reading can bring to you. I would like to thank you for all that you did for me. I appreciate you very much."

Later on in the year, he sent me a picture of a page in his book and wrote:

"Hi Mrs. Mantz. I was going through a box of my old stuff, and I came across the books I wrote in English class. I thought I'd share this picture with you. Those books were fun to write."

Teaching at the high school level in special education was different from working at the elementary level. First, high school teachers were mavericks, doing their own thing in their classrooms. Roma, the no-nonsense department chair, was a resource for me as was the teacher next door, Mr. Bradley. We joked that we were both so loud, we could hear one another teaching through the walls. We would cover each other's classes for bathroom breaks when needed, attended one another's IEPs, and often complain about the paperwork overload in special education.

A day in my school life was never the same, but it could have running themes. On a Monday, I would start students off with a review of their weekend homework, which was typically a journal assignment. If I got fifty percent participation, that was pretty decent. I would then give them a fifteen-minute quick write on a topic (This assignment connected to the readings we would do later in the week). As they scribbled down their thoughts using a bubble map, I walked around the room as the paraeducator stepped outside and called parents of students who did their homework; the kids liked this as it rewarded rather than punished.

As the class wrote, I printed out my own piece that I had written the night before. I chose to write a song using my name. "Oh Jackie, oh Jackie, I knew a girl Jackie was her name, since I started teaching, I've never been the same as I love my job, without teaching where would I be? Where would I be? I knew a girl who was once like you. She hated school and thought she was cool, but she found higher learning and now teaching is all she wants to do." I sang it to the class. They applauded even as they groaned. I write and teach from my heart. I was not afraid to make a fool of myself by singing a cappella in my class even though I sounded like an alley cat.

What did I get in return? One student wrote a rap about being a black boy who loved his name, but due to his past, he felt he was living a life in vain. I learned that one female student thought her name and body were ugly. A kid wrote how he was named after a loved one who had passed on. Almost all read their words haltingly and smiled as I passed out Jolly Rancher candies after we listened and snapped our approval. This is why I teach.

The years went by so fast. In 2010, I met and married the love of my life, Joe Rodriguez. We got our dog, Elizabeth Barrett Browning, Lizzy. Life and teaching during those years were a joy.

Final Gap

On April 25th, 2010, we were married. We drove to Las Vegas, ate pancakes, and scribbled down our vows on napkins sticky with syrup. "We eloped and were married by Elvis in Las Vegas," I always laughingly tell people when they ask about our wedding. I recall our Priceline-inspired choice of accommodations at Hooters, followed by an evening at *The Lion King* show. The next day, we drove home, newlyweds. Some of our loved ones, including family members, students, and colleagues, witnessed our union via online streaming.

"Is this for real?" someone asked.

Joe and I have stayed together through some challenging times, but we have always been *por vida.* Just last summer, we tattooed identical hibiscus flowers on our wrists along with the date, 4/25/2010. It's a lighthearted nod to Joe's initial surprise upon learning of my tattoos, when he remarked, "I didn't know teachers could have tattoos." I didn't know how Joe's love would fill in the gaps of my life, cementing a life into balance. I now know.

A Smile and a Wave

Some students with disabilities required more support than others in class. Herman could have been placed in a moderate to severe setting by high school, but his mom wanted him to stay in the least restrictive environment (LRE). She advocated for him to remain in a more academically focused setting. Herman taught me many lessons.

Herman had a smile that lit up a room. His laugh echoed across the walls of my classroom, encouraging reciprocal kindness from even the toughest kids. Herman had a slightly square head due to having had hydrocephalus as a child. One green eye sagged, and his mouth struggled to pronounce words. Herman's mom made sure he looked preppy in striped polo shirts and ironed slacks. Herman loved to hear books, stories, and writings of authors aloud. He would ask questions and listen. He would write all his notes slowly into a notebook. Herman was scared when he first came to high school and hid under his desk the first day we met. I watched as he held his head in his hands and rocked back and forth.

"I want to go home, loud and bright," he mumbled over and over. I turned down the lights and music.

"Herman, can you sit with me? We can read together," I said. He took my hand and got up slowly. No one laughed at him that day. Karla walked over to Herman as he sat with me. He read the text easily from the middle school book I took off the silent reading shelf. But he didn't understand any questions I asked him about the story. Karla came up to my desk and asked, "Can Herman read with me? He reads well."

Herman loved to write. At first, he wrote simple sentences. After a few months, he began to flourish, painstakingly adding words to his simple sentences until he was writing paragraphs. He would read his writings aloud to the class in a full voice, and we would always snap our fingers in approval as a huge smile spread across his face. Karla became Herman's peer tutor. She could check any kid with a look. Her makeup was as heavy as she was slim. Her big golden hoop earrings dangled flirtatiously. All the boys in the class had a crush on her. She loved to wear all her gold as it matched her honey blond hair and tan skin. Herman and Karla would gossip and giggle in Spanish. They would stop their *chisme* whenever I walked by and start reading again. Karla and Herman became close friends. She was able to coax him into a chair by sitting with him during group time. Herman was a hard worker, the hardest worker in the class. His humor tipped the scales back into alignment. Herman could get people to laugh just with a look.

"Ms. M, want to hear my story?" asked Herman.

"Read it to the class," I said.

"Okay, so once upon a time, I saw a cat with gray fur. She was a magic cat with kittens. They drank from her and climbed over to get milk. I named her Dulce," said Herman.

"Let's give Herman some snaps! Who has a question?" I asked.

"How old was Dulce when you got her?" Karla asked.

"She was a baby," answered Herman.

Herman stayed at our high school program until the quarter before graduation. He was then eligible for the Adult Transition Program (ATP). To attend ATP, Herman had to enroll in a moderate to severe program and receive a high school certificate of completion rather than a diploma. I remember the last day I saw Herman. He came up to me, smiled, and hugged me.

"Ms. M, I will miss you and writing. Say bye to your dog Lizzy. She was fun to hang out with at lunch. I won't forget you." With that, Herman was gone. I taught him for all four years at the high school. It was sad at the beginning of the next school year when he was not sitting in his regular seat. But, I wished him well and knew he had a wonderful family to support him. I did not see Herman for two years. I saw his mom though at the local Del Taco where she worked. I always asked his her about him, and she would tell me, "A Herman le está yendo bien en su nueva escuela," when she handed me my bean burrito with extra cheese and secret sauce.

The next school year, Karla, Herman's former helper, was my teacher's assistant, and we laughed and nodded as we fondly remembered Herman's antics. Karla never spoke a harsh word about her friends. She was also vocal about wanting children. Right before winter break, Karla and some students received a betta fish from Mr. Rose as a prize. She accidentally killed it by shaking the bag too much. Karla let the tears fall and said, "I'm so sorry." Many of my students stay in touch with me via Facebook after graduation. It has been around ten years since Karla graduated. She is now married and has two lovely boys.

Karla would often visit my classroom for lunch with her best friend, Starr. I would play *Star Wars* movies for them and allow kids to eat lunch in our room as long as they listened when I said, "Don't make a mess. I'm not your maid." Karla and Starr were hilarious and regaled me with stories of their work and dating lives. Karla worked at McDonald's. She had practiced counting money and giving change with Mr. Bradley, the high school special education math teacher, before she started working. Starr worked at Shakey's Pizza. Joe and I would go visit her on the weekends to eat pepperoni pizza and mojo potatoes. Karla and Starr would stroll into the classroom with their school lunches in hand, sit near my desk, and talk to me while the movie played.

One day, Starr looked me in the eye, eyebrow cocked, and said, "Ms. Mantz, that boy was cheap. He didn't even offer me popcorn at the movies, and we had to go to the matinee. Do you have any popcorn?"

"That's a red flag. Nothing worse than a stingy person," I said and pulled a bag of popcorn out of my snack drawer to give to her. I always had snacks for the kids. I kept it simple: popcorn, Wonder Bread, and peanut butter and jelly. If a kid was hungry, they got fed. Kids have a hard time learning if their stomachs are rumbling. This was before the days of universal free breakfast and lunch. Back then, free lunch required paperwork similar to student loan docs. Many parents would come to me, and we would fill the pages out together. Others did not. Why didn't parents fill out the paperwork so their kids could eat? Some of my parents were Spanish speakers. Others may have had learning disabilities or had been in special education themselves. Some parents were scared of immigration authorities finding out about their undocumented status. Others were working two to three jobs just trying to survive. Some families were too proud to accept any help, so their kids brought their lunches. Ms. Roma collected the parts of the school lunch kids didn't eat and kept them in her fridge for kids who were hungry. We found a way.

A couple of years after Herman left my class and moved to the Adult Transition Program (ATP), I decided to teach Extended School Year (ESY) in the summer for the moderate to severe program known today as Functional Life Skills (FLS). I did not have a moderate to severe credential, but any special education teacher could teach ESY.

Our schedule was from 9 a.m. to 1 p.m. The day went by fast. I would get to work at 8:30 a.m., write down the schedule on the board in different-colored Expo markers, and lay the journals on the desks. Because these students were lower-level readers and writers, I adapted my writing opener. All students need an opportunity to write about their experiences. I would type out a prompt like, "What makes you happy?" Then I would create a word bank to support them in their writing. For kids who needed more support, I would create sentence frames, and they could fill in one or two words. They always illustrated their writing. Writing just a few sentences could take up to thirty minutes. When we were done, students would use the microphone to read their writings aloud.

"It makes me happy to come to school. I love karaoke, reading, and eating lunch," Joey, one of the best writers and singers in the class, said in a booming voice.

"My dogs make me happy," said Michelle haltingly into the microphone, prompted by the aide in the class. All kids participated, even if they just drew a picture instead of words.

After writing, the students read stories at their levels for fifteen minutes. Then I read them a book like *Holes*, and at the end, I would ask them some questions. Then we did math. Most of the students were still working on computation, so we would play games and sing multiplication songs to help them memorize their math facts. By this time, we'd take a break and then have physical education. We'd walk outside and get some fresh air and play some kickball. After P.E., each student was encouraged to choose a song to sing. I will never forget Carlos who always sang "Eye of the Tiger." He knew all the words and would put on a show in front of the class like he was performing at the Grammys. After karaoke, we would mix it up doing a variety of lessons in science, art, and social studies. Then it was time to go home.

This program was when I first saw Herman again. Halfway through the first week, I saw him lining up for the bus at the end of the day. "Hi Herman! How's summer school?" He looked at me and smiled and waved as he got on the bus. I tried again the next day when I saw him getting off the bus to come to school. "Hi Herman!" He nodded at me and smiled. "Herman, do you remember me?" I asked. "Ms. Mantz," he said in a soft voice. "Herman, how is your mom? Is she still working at Del Taco? Can you use your words, Herman? Herman, do you remember me?" I said. "Ms. Mantz," he said in a soft voice. "Herman, Karla says hi and so does Starr. We always talk about you," I said. His eyes lit up, and a huge smile spread across his face. He waved goodbye as his class went into the school.

Every day Herman waved to me when he saw me, and I spoke to him, but I never had a conversation with him like the ones we had when he was in a high school classroom where speech was everywhere. In his new setting, Herman was the highest performer academically. He did not have the constant peer modeling of language. I struggled coming to terms with Herman's regression. Maybe he was more verbal in Spanish at home? I still wonder how he is doing. At twenty-two years old, students “age out” of special educational services. Herman had a wonderful supportive mom and siblings. I know he was safe and cared for, but I pray someone is having him talk and write. Herman’s voice and stories matter.

Searching for True Faith

I am moving to the recent past for a moment. Last year, I read *Between the World and Me* by Ta-Nehisi Coates with students in senior seminar at the continuation school where I currently teach as a general education teacher. The class was organic in parts, growing for nine weeks in the soil of the students' needs. We read this book for typical reasons. It was a number one *New York Times* bestseller, winner of the 2015 National Book Award for nonfiction, and written in epistolary form. The story is narrated in a series of letters to Coates' son. The students also wrote their own personal statements. We read this book because I was inspired to teach more writers of color by a student I taught during those years I taught high school special education. Some students stay in your mind and lie on your soul, inspiring you to do more. True Faith was one of those students.

"I'm a poet, don't you know it," said True Faith to me with a lopsided smile and a nod. He carried the book he had created in the special education high school English class I taught in 2013 at the comprehensive high school. True Faith was a natural leader. He had swag and street smarts, a type of intelligence we underrate in the educational system. He was stylish and sported baggy sweatshirts emblazoned with Tupac quotes. His hair always looked as if he had just gone to the barber with his fresh and so clean fade. I look back and feel ashamed that I was so surprised when I realized True Faith could read and write above grade level. He had qualified for special education services under other health impaired (OHI). He was diagnosed with

ADHD, so he took the tenth-grade English class with students who, on average, read at a third-grade level and struggled to write a paragraph. For struggling writers, learning to write is a challenging and complex task. There were always a few students in the classes I taught that would make me shake my head and wonder, How did they qualify? I'm not a psychologist, but I had years of experience working with struggling learners; True Faith devoured stories. His honest, thoughtful writing flew out of his fingers. He liked to write his pieces then type them into a Word document. I shook my head at an educational system that had put this gifted reader and writer into a special education setting.

True Faith had a lot going on. He was placed in foster care at a young age but was later reunited with his mother. He was labeled a behavior problem by other teachers. He had a hard time staying still. Yet, when he was into something, he could focus. True Faith had a brother, Jayvon, who was also enrolled in my class, but he was like a bird, always flying around the school. True Faith sometimes missed class too, but I always made sure to acknowledge him in the morning. He and I both knew that when I saw him at school, he was expected to come to class.

"Ms. Mantz, can we look at Tupac's songs in class as, man, that homie goes deep." True Faith typically used the N word with the "a" ending. One day, we had a deep conversation on the history of the "N" word, so he tried not to use it in class. He wrote about love, loss, grief, fear, racial prejudice, and his life. His poems were more like songs as he modeled them on the rappers he listened to, which included my favorite, Eminem.

"For a white guy, Eminem is all right." When we read the ending of *Of Mice and Men*, True Faith stayed after class with me to discuss the death of Lennie by George.

"George did the right thing. Curly would have tortured him. Remember the dog that the old guy loved? He was so pissed that he let someone else put him down. Lennie couldn't go down like that. I'd do the same for Jayvon." All year we wrote poems, songs, stories, letters, raps, rants, and essays for their book project.

True Faith charmed fellow talented artist students to draw illustrations for each one of his pieces since he disliked drawing. His book used every page. By then, I had a class set of laptop computers with Microsoft Word. Every student who needed to print had to save their work on a memory stick. Each student had their own yellow-and-white memory stick thanks to a district grant. Printing student work was my least favorite part. Mr. Robertson printed out student work for me so I could handwrite suggestions. I usually only had time to do one review of a student's pieces, and that was fine with most kids. True Faith was detail-oriented, and he enjoyed the revision process.

"I found a few more errors. Mr. Robertson, can you help me out and print it again?" True Faith knew the power of a well-edited piece of writing. His poems and essays frequently adorned the back wall behind my desk. I wish I'd kept these poems and essays. If we had completed this project with today's technology, I could find the golden words he'd written as a young man and send them to him, if I could find him.

True Faith only stayed at the high school for one year. He moved. It was a couple of years later when I heard his name mentioned again. Mr. Bradley asked me, "Did you teach that one kid and his brother who had that strange name? It had faith in it."

"Are you talking about True Faith? Yes, I taught him and the brother. Why?" I asked.

"He's on trial for strong-arm robbery. Another statistic," Mr. Bradley said. I looked at my friend and sighed.

"True Faith was a talented writer." I walked away. These were the times I felt the divide between me and the other teachers. Some teachers didn't get it. Mr. Bradley and I were friends. The next day he hugged me and said, "I'm sorry, I know you cared about True Faith." I was sorry we lived in a world where kids like True Faith disappeared and then reappeared in my mind's eye to haunt and inspire me.

True Faith was a young man with hopes, dreams, and talent. In *Between the World and Me*, Ta-Nehisi Coates writes, "In accepting both the chaos of history and the fact of my total end, I was freed to consider how I wished to live—specifically, how do I live free in this black body?" (12). I wish True Faith had had a chance to read this book. I don't know where he is today, but if you are out there, dear, I saw you. I heard you, and I valued your voice and stories. Every time I write about a student, I remember. I remember all of the many students I worked with through my years teaching at the high school. I know what we did mattered in Room 228.

I would like to take a moment to remember the principal I call Wilson Worth in this book. He always did what was right for kids. This unforgettable man always supported me and our students. Today, I was reminded of the call and response he would yell out at assemblies and staff meetings: "What time is it? Game Time!" when I attended his celebration of life with many of my former colleagues. At the end of the remembrance, his daughter told us, "If you want to honor my dad, lead with love." I do.

The Land of 228

Tim walked into Room 228, his black spiky hair shaking back and forth. Tim's finger was curled downward as if he were missing a finger. He spoke in a nasal approximation of his teacher's voice.

Mr. Rose said, "Stop, Tim. You need to stop that now. You can leave the classroom if you're going to keep on." Tim pointed his curled finger at me, reminding me that Mr. Rose was missing a finger. Then his voice suddenly changed back to his own. "Here I am, Ms. Mantz, back to the other dummies."

Tim was the best golf player at our high school and also in special education classes. He wore a turquoise Lacoste polo shirt, peach shorts, and pristine white sneakers. He looked like he was ready to go to the driving range.

I did not answer him. It was best not to react and then praise him when he did something positive. So I gave him no attention, yet. Tim clumped over to the back of the class near the back door where a huge bookshelf blocked a view of the students and sat down at a desk. He put his hands over his head.

"Thanks, Tim, for sitting down," I said.

"You're welcome, Ms. Pants," he said in a flat voice.

We continued working on our "Dark Christmas" stories inspired by *Santaland Diaries* by David Sedaris. Keynon struggled with writing in class. He wrote at a first-grade level. As I roamed around the room helping students complete the bubble maps on their stories, Mr. Robertson sat by Keynon, prompting him to write a word in each bubble about the plot, characters, setting, and theme of his story idea. Keynon was identified as having an intellectual disability.

Ricardo, a student on the autism spectrum, sat with a stuffed animal on his head. Taco the turtle was his best friend. He carefully filled out a bubble map. I looked over his shoulder and saw the words "MURDEROUS SANTA CLAUS" written in green in the character's bubble. In the setting's bubble, the words "OH UNHOLY NIGHT" written in red. I smiled as Ricardo looked up at me, patted his back, and gave him a thumbs up. Ricardo was into horror movies, and it was reflected in his writings. Keynon looked around the room.

"Tim, want to help me with this writing thing we gotta do? Ms. Mantz said we could do it with partners. I know Mr. Rose is an asshole barf bag, but we gotta keep going, dude. I know you can write and draw, and I got some ideas," he said. Where did Keynon get this stuff? His words were inappropriate yet inspirational.

Tim put his head up and shouted, "Can it have a zombie theme?"

"Anything, man, I'm desperate here. You know, we have to pass all four years of this English class. Ms. Mantz says I have to do this damn book thing. I got the cover and drawings done, but I need stories," pleaded Keynon.

Tim's professional-level art and writings on *The Walking Dead* were posted among other students' work on the bright bulletin boards that had "PROLIFIC WORKS" emblazoned across the top. Tim was diagnosed with autism and Tourette's syndrome. He had facial tics. He swore a lot too, but this was not a symptom of his Tourette's as he used profanity with discretion. Tim was obsessed with the comic book series. He wrote fan fiction. I had watched the television series, but I was not a fan of the comic books. Keynon looked up at me and smiled as Tim sat beside him. I walked around the room and sat next to Frankie, who had his head on the desk.

"Not today, Ms. Mantz, not today," he said in a tired voice.

"It's all good, Frankie. Just checking in," I said. Having Frankie even here at school was a breakthrough when he was going through one of his depressive episodes.

Keynon and Tim sat huddled together, whispering. "All it has to have is a story set around a winter theme? We could set the story during Christmas. Which characters do you want in it?" "Could I be in it? Sure, you could be a zombie. We got this, Key. Move over, Mr. Robertson, go help, Stephanie."

Mr. Robertson, in his typically serene way, laughed, got up, and walked away from the dynamic duo. He sat down next to Stephanie, who had her head in her hands and whispered softly to herself, "I don't know what to do."

"Now, Ms. Stephanie, where does your story take place? Remember, you chose to write about Christmas, so where does Santa Claus hang out?" Mr. Robertson had a way of pulling ideas from students who were struggling with writing. He would scribe as they spoke. Stephanie said, "The North Pole." He wrote it down and continued filling out the bubble map with Stephanie. She giggled as he drew humorous stick figures next to every bubble.

The door of the classroom flew open, and Maleah strode into the room. "Those motherfucking security guards are after me again, Ms. Mantz. I was just using the restroom. They are stalking me. I'm going to put in a complaint against them." Maleah's braids swung back and forth as she looked at Keynon and said, "Keep your eyes to yourself, little man."

"We're cool, Maleah. I know about them security as they put me down hard the other day. Thinking I'm fronting them and shit," Keynon replied. Earlier in the week, the school's security officer explained to me what happened.

"Ms. Mantz, Keynon was throwing up gang signs and threatening us. We didn't know he was special." "Special" was the term people used about the students in my class. Recently, I visited a special education middle school classroom to observe one of our new teachers. I was exhausted after an hour. Now that I teach at a continuation high school, I sometimes forget how exhausting teaching day in and day out in a special education classroom could be. I don't regret those years, but I don't want to go back to them either. Maybe I am getting older and tire more easily. Truthfully, I cannot fathom having to do all the IEPs and teaching all day. But special education teachers do it. Maybe this is why there is such a special education teacher shortage.

Recently, a fellow teacher told me, "You know Tim's mom and I are friends. She taught with me for years. She told me, 'Jackie loved Tim despite the extreme behavior. She taught him and loved him through it all.'" She said this to me, after an AA meeting of all times. I cried. I do love all of my students, and I try never to give up on kids. But there were days I wanted, I needed, a break from the students.

The student Maleah in the story used to call me a "fat bitch" all the time. I knew it wasn't about me. She had mental health issues. But, after dealing with her verbal abuse for months, I was resentful. My assistant principal at the time, Mr. Saguaro, put Maeleah in another class for a week after I told him I didn't know if I wanted to continue teaching as I felt so guilty for being angry. He listened, talked to Maleah, and she was not allowed to go to my class for a week while I worked on letting it go. She apologized, we moved on, and she and I developed a strong bond after the incident. But teachers are human and have feelings. Mr. Saguaro's intervention allowed me time to process my own resentment, and I stayed teaching. What would have happened if my administrator had ignored me or made me feel even more guilty for my honesty?

My former student Tim now lives at home with his mom. He is living a quiet life going to church. He no longer golfs as his grandfather, who was his mentor, died. But we all stop doing certain things that no longer serve us. I used to run marathons and complete triathlons. Now I do yoga. We all change and grow.

People with disabilities are people first, so why would I feel sorry for Tim or Maleah? This is a form of unconscious bias that serves no one. We should not feel sorry for people with disabilities. All of us need to get to know one another's stories so we can understand how to better support each other.

School district staff need more training regarding students with disabilities. I currently present to district staff on unconscious bias. The bias against students with disabilities is extreme. Students in special education graduate at a much lower rate than their peers in general education. The graduation rates for students with behavioral issues in special education are even lower. In my years of teaching, general education teachers have said to me on numerous occasions, "I don't want those kids in my class." All teachers, both in special education and general education, have said, "I didn't know your kids could write so well." Teachers historically have lower expectations for students with disabilities than their non-disabled peers. Teachers have said, "Oh, you must have so much patience to be a special education teacher." I am no saint, nor savior.

As a general education teacher currently, I support students with disabilities within my classroom setting. I support all students and work with all students. What benefits one, benefits all. Here's another student's story I remember from my high school years. It deals with my own bias.

Star Student

Alora was my pick for star student. During the first few weeks of the school year, she would often place her head on the desk and do nothing. Alora was in my ninth-grade English class and participated in special education classes at the high school due to her qualifying disability of emotional disturbance. In the class, she had not uttered a word beyond "here" for two weeks. She simply pushed all the work forward on the desk when I handed it to her. Alora had long, straight auburn hair, full cheeks, and a perpetual scowl. Occasionally, I would hear her mutter words in Tagalog, swearing passive-aggressively to the room. I wish I had had Google Translator back then.

During one of our special education department meetings, the department chair, Roma, and the school psychologist, Shelly, decided that each staff member would choose a struggling student to mentor. Alora was an obvious choice as she was failing all her classes.

I observed Alora as she doodled and wrote in a notebook. I approached her and asked, “So, you like to draw and write?”

“Maybe I do, but only on some days,” she replied.

Our class continued to work on our book project. I decided to show *The Freedom Writers* movie to the class. Alora was riveted. Beneath her sneer, she had a sense of humor. She began to open up and work tirelessly on the cover of her book. I vividly remember the Pegasus she had drawn flying into the sun. Alora even started doing her makeup in class.

"Black eyeliner makes me look like Trinity from *The Matrix*," she said. Alora began dating Pedro. They would walk in holding hands. Then one day, Pedro was in tears.

"I don't like him. He is too clingy," said Alora. By the end of the year, Alora passed most of her classes. She started hanging out with Tiffany and Jessica. As the end of the year approached, we had Alora's IEP. Then it was summer.

"Bye, Ms. Mantz. See you next year," Alora said.

"See you soon, Alora," I replied, waving goodbye.

On the first day of the new school year, a stocky student walked into our classroom with black, spiky hair, dressed all in black. He had black eyeliner, just like Alora used to wear. Wait, that was Alora.

"Hi, Ms. Mantz, are you ready for a wild and crazy year?" asked Alora.

"Yes, Alora, I am," I said slowly, looking away.

"Umm, Ms. Mantz, can you call me Neo?" Alora asked.

"Like from the movie *Matrix*? Uh, yeah, I guess. What happened? You look so different. Is everything okay, Alora? I'm sorry, Neo," I said, stumbling over my words. I didn't understand how a kid could change so suddenly. Where was this coming from?

"I'm being me, Ms. Mantz. This is me," said Neo.

"Okay, so I guess you won't be painting your nails anymore, huh," I joked. Neo walked out of the class. I called, "Neo, wait," but he was gone. For the next few weeks, Neo put his head down on the desk in class and refused to do work. I finally called a meeting with Neo's mom.

Neo sat with his head on the desk as Mom and I made small talk. Then I told her about Neo's struggles. Before the meeting, I asked Neo what he wanted me to call him in front of his mom.

"It doesn't matter. I go by Neo and Alora. It depends. My mom knows. She loves me," said Neo with an accusing look.

As we sat down at the classroom table, I noticed Neo had his head on the desk. I decided to get right to it.

"Neo has been struggling lately," I said. "He won't do any work in class. He's failing all of his classes," I said to Neo's mom. She looked at me and then looked at Neo. She nudged his shoulder, and Neo sat up.

"Neo is going through changes. Now she is a tomboy. I don't care. I just want her to graduate high school. She doesn't want to be a caregiver like me. It's hard work," said Neo's mom.

"I hear you. Neo won't talk to me or do any work in class. He's failing," I said.

"You don't like me anymore." Neo lifted his head and looked me in the eyes.

"Neo, I still like you," I said.

"You don't talk to me anymore. Ever since I changed my dress and hair, you've ignored me," he said.

"I'm sorry, Neo, I was surprised. Maybe I did get uncomfortable. But I want you to be your most authentic self," I said.

"Neo, Ms. Mantz still likes you. It's all in your head. Look, she's here talking with us. If she didn't care, she wouldn't try to talk. Here, Ms. Mantz, we eat now. I bought Suman Malagkit for us," said Neo's mom. She brought out napkins and placed a couple of banana leaves in front of all of us. As we unwrapped the leaves, the aroma of sweet coconut rice wafted up our noses, and we all smiled.

"Okay, Ms. Mantz, I will finish my book. I know you want to read it," said Neo.

"California Education Code Section 220 prohibits discrimination on the basis of gender identity and gender expression—in addition to sexual orientation and other protected characteristics—in public schools or non-religious private schools. This means that a school must respect a transgender or gender nonconforming student's gender identity and/or expression." (ACLU of Southern California, 2023)

I struggled back then when a student transitioned from female to male, but I learned a lot from the experience. Today, I ask students on the first day of class to fill out a card. On the front of the card, they write their name and preferred pronouns. I practice pronouncing their names and call them by the names they prefer. If I make a mistake, I apologize and do better. Creating an inclusive environment where all students feel respected and valued is crucial, and asking for preferred pronouns is a simple yet effective way to show respect for individuals' gender identities. Apologizing and correcting mistakes when using incorrect pronouns demonstrates a commitment to creating a supportive atmosphere for all students. A proactive approach on the first day of class sets a positive tone and fosters a sense of inclusion. Continuing to prioritize inclusivity and understanding in our teaching practices will undoubtedly make a significant difference in the lives of all students.

Right?

You have the right
to be called by the pronouns you use
to use the restroom of your gender identity
to participate in team sports, to be free from bullying
to be your authentic self, to feel safe—
Right?

82% have considered suicide, 40% attempted
fleeing from discrimination, violence, religious persecution
scared to even tell family, might be harmed, put out on the streets.

We must, for our children's children, listen rather than speak
it is all of our struggle, a struggle to love, love without conditions
amplify voices before our own, when one suffers, we all suffer—
we know this is right, right?

Neo did not graduate from high school; he dropped out and went to work in retail. Then he tried working as a home care support provider with his mom and that did not work out. A few weeks later he found a job at a grocery store. He worked in the deli for a couple of years. I called to check up on Neo, and he told me they fired him for throwing ham at a customer who was rude to him. Neo and I still chat on Facebook occasionally. He has a girlfriend who lives in the Philippines and wants to move there to be with her. Pedro, Neo's ex-boyfriend, is married and the proud father of three children: one boy and two girls.

Public Displays of Affection

I stay in touch with many former students. I was Wilma's teacher all four years of high school. She graduated in 2011. Whenever Wilma is in town, we grab lunch together. After graduation, Wilma moved to Riverside to live in a group home.

Last year, Wilma and her boyfriend, Steve, went to lunch with Joe and me. We picked them up at the group home in Riverside where Wilma lived. Steve was in his thirties and still lived with his parents, but Wilma's mom had pushed for her to live with others her age in a supported environment.

Wilma and Steve walked outside to our car. Wilma had curled her long brown hair and had gone heavy on the pink glitter eyeshadow. She wore a pretty floral skirt and top. Steve's hair was cut military-style, and he wore a button-up shirt and dress pants.

"Hey, Ms. Mantz, this is Steve, my boyfriend. Steve, this is Ms. Mantz and her husband, Joe," Wilma said in a loud voice.

"I'm Mr. Mantz"—Joe extended his hand toward Steve—"but you can call me Joe. The last name's Rodriguez, but don't let that fool you. My wife's a feminist." Joe chuckled, winking his right eye.

"You're funny, Joe." Wilma said.

We went to eat lunch at the Spaghetti Factory. Wilma and Steve had their arms all over one another and kissed between bites of food. Joe and I averted our eyes. The couple at the next table stared at them. I gave them a dirty look.

"Wilma, want to go to the ladies' room?" I asked.

"Sure, I could reapply my lipstick," said Wilma.

When Wilma and I went to the restroom, Wilma said, "Steve and I are going to have sex, Ms. Mantz. My mom knows." I nodded and said, "Wilma, you and Steve have the right to make this decision in your relationship. I am glad you sought advice from your mom though. Also, you might want to lay off the kissing when you are at a restaurant," I advised.

"Ohhh, my mom told me that too when Steve and I went to dinner with her," Wilma replied. "I forgot."

Later, after we dropped them off and drove back home, Joe and I laughed together. "Well, they have just as much a right to 'do it' as anyone else," I said. "Yes, but I don't want to watch them make out while eating spaghetti," he replied.

Recently, Wilma turned thirty years old. Her mom threw her a party. There were pink heart-shaped glasses, a dessert table, carne asada, and lots of booze. Wilma was the belle of the ball in her red dress and pink heels. She had lots of glittery eye shadow on too. All her friends from her group home sat at a table with her and drank strawberry margaritas. Even the owner of the group home was there sipping on a cocktail.

"Ms. Mantz, you don't drink, right? I remember. That's why we have sparkling water and cranberry juice. My gramps doesn't drink either," Wilma said.

"Thanks, Wilma, I appreciate the mocktail," I replied.

"Ms. Mantz was my teacher for all four years of English. We wrote books together. My mom still has mine." Wilma yelled across the room, "Mom, can you go get my book I wrote with Ms. Mantz?" Wilma's mom brought the book out a few minutes later and said, "Wilma, remember, we don't need to yell. You can walk over and ask me nicely." The young people *oohed* and *aahed* as they passed around the book, ate tacos, and sipped their drinks. Wilma showed off her ring.

"Steve and I are engaged," said Wilma.

"When is the wedding? Why isn't Steve here?" I inquired.

"Well, it's a long story. He couldn't get a ride. His mom was supposed to bring him," Wilma took a long gulp from her margarita. "He's a mama's boy," she said, and the entire table giggled.

Wilma's group home relocated to San Diego so they could all live closer to the beach. I called Wilma after I saw her relationship status on Facebook had been changed to single.

"It was so frustrating. He wanted me to move back to Riverside to be near him, but if I leave my group home, I can't move back. He wouldn't put in a job transfer with Amazon to San Diego."

"Do you two talk anymore?" I asked.

"No, because all we do is fight. His mom got into it too. She told me to stop calling him. Then he had the nerve to say his mom loved me. I didn't feel loved," Wilma answered.

"Did you give back the ring," I asked.

"Nope, we were together eight years. I told him I was keeping the ring. He said okay," she boasted.

"Well just be careful out there in the dating scene," I cautioned.

"Don't worry, I'm just going for tacos and beer. Delsey, my house mom, is coming with me. I am still on the rebound, but this guy is cute. He is only a year older than me and drives.

"I also want to get my driver's license. Now all I need to do is talk to my controlling mom. She worries too much about me," Wilma said.

Despite the challenges she has faced, Wilma is embracing life and happily living at the beach house working at SeaWorld. She is single and going on dates using Facebook Singles.

"I've had heartbreak, but I know I'll find love," Wilma said. "I'm not giving up. But, I won't stop living my life."

Home and Hospital Years

In my first eight years of teaching, I didn't take on any extra duties. I was too occupied with learning how to be an effective teacher. When I moved to the high school level in the Coachella Valley, I was in my eighth year of teaching. At the beginning of my second year at the high school, my mentor, Roma, encouraged me to support students in home and hospital schooling. Home and hospital schooling entails five hours a week of instruction in a one-to-one setting in the students' home or at a neutral location. This was before Zoom, so we would always visit students' homes to teach them or meet them at the library after our regular school day. Only recently have I ceased working with children in home and hospital settings. Time has become my most precious resource as I age. Over the fifteen years I've worked in the Coachella Valley, I've assisted numerous kids on home and hospital schooling. Some, like Frankie, were only in home and hospital for a short period.

Frankie and I were acquainted from his time in my class at the high school. His mom called for an IEP meeting, resulting in him being placed on home and hospital schooling due to medical reasons. Now, a doctor's authorization is required for home and hospital schooling, but in the past, an IEP team could make that decision. Frankie met me at the library a few hours after my school day twice a week. Karl Mark, the coordinator of special education services, had called me.

"Can you work with Frankie on home and hospital?" he asked.

"Sure, okay. As long as we can meet at a neutral location, as I know his mom, she likes to leave. I can't be at home with him alone," I said. It's a sad reality that teachers have to protect themselves and establish boundaries in such situations. I had this policy because some parents would attempt to leave me alone with their child. I had to politely inform them that I was leaving if they were leaving. So, we met at the library, and I had all the necessary materials for him. However, Frankie showed no interest in the StudySync materials on leadership, the history of the world, or the science of the earth. He grimaced when I held up the algebra math book, as did I, and shrugged.

"What do you want to learn, Frankie?" I asked. I felt like Tom Cruise in the movie *Jerry Maguire*: "Help me, help you."

"Can we learn about being a good father? My girlfriend is pregnant," he said. His girlfriend was my former student too.

"Sure, Frankie. Let's find some resources here," I replied. During our time in the library, he diligently learned about fatherhood through our readings and online research. As his teacher, I had to adapt the learning to Frankie. In home and hospital instruction, just like in a classroom, one had to foster a supportive learning environment. Education extends beyond traditional academic subjects; it encompasses life skills and personal development. We went through the shelves and found a book titled *The Expectant Father*. I had no idea if the book was any good, but it was a *New York Times* bestseller according to the book's cover. Frankie read it aloud to me, slowly and deliberately, his knees shaking. He improved his reading comprehension in our sessions. He was also studying science and math by doing lessons on child development and the cost of raising a child. All these materials could also be found on the library's shelves. Our lessons reminded me of my first years of teaching.

Frankie met me for a month, and I felt as if we had been making progress. Then, Monday morning, Karl called me again.

"Frankie is gone. He ran away when he learned his mom was going to send him to a group home." I wish I could have worked with Frankie longer. His abrupt departure underscores the unpredictable paths a student may take. Frankie is out there somewhere in the world today. I hope he is in his child's life.

Another student I'll never forget is Justin. He was in home and hospital due to severe health issues. He was non-verbal and had been in medically fragile classrooms for years. However, his health had deteriorated to the point where he needed schooling at home. His mom was a nurse. She was also a single mom. Justin had two brothers and an older sister. They all participated in Justin's care. Mary could not care for him alone, as his needs were extensive. She had nurses coming in too, but many times it was the brother or sister who would reposition him or move him if needed. I loved how his brothers and sister would joke with him when they came into the room. I taught Justin at home and hospital for years. Here is one day I vividly remember.

What Makes You Beautiful

Justin was lying in his bed, propped up by pillows, when I walked into the bright yellow and blue room. The television was playing a *Star Wars* cartoon. I walked over and shut it off. Justin had on his blue and yellow smock. His mouth opened wide into a grin, and he said, "Arghhhhh." The machine beeped twice. Justin was on his back, and his legs were propped up with foam triangles. Wrapped around each of his thighs was a black rubber band. The outward side was Velcro, and there was a white square attached. In the middle of the white square was a colored button. One button was red, and one was green. These buttons were Justin's voice. Dean, the adaptive technology teacher, would come to see Justin too. He recorded messages using his voice. Justin's goal was to hit the buttons to communicate during our teaching sessions.

"Breathe, Justin," I said, echoing the words his mom said to remind him to breathe. "How are you, Justin? It's good to see you." He hit the green button on his right leg. "I had a good day." I smiled.

"That's awesome, Justin," I said. "Dean was here today. That's his voice. Did you know Dean and I are friends?" As I spoke to Justin, I readied for class. I opened up my log on Google. Then I grabbed the bubble machine and the pink poodle, both switch activated. Another way Justin practiced his communication was by activating these toys through deliberate head movement.

"How was your day, Dr. Mantz?" asked Justin by pressing the red pre-recorded button on his left leg. I knew Justin was cognizant of me, but I was not entirely sure how much he truly understood due to the severe nature of his disabilities. But I always answered as if he was fully aware of what he was asking by pushing the button.

"My day was great, Justin. We made Valentine's poems. Do you want to make your mom a card?" Justin's eyes darted back and forth. He struggled to maintain eye contact, but he could do it for a few seconds. Our eyes met, and we smiled. I wiped the drool off the corner of his mouth with a small hand towel. He stuck his tongue out and moved his head back and forth. I could feel Justin communicating with me through his eyes and vocalizations. I knew he was in there and just wanted to be acknowledged and seen by me. It was a lot, though, some nights to stay present and engaged with Justin.

"Are you talking about me, Justin?" Mary, Justin's mom, came over and patted my arm.

"Do you need anything?" Mary asked.

"We're good. Justin is ready to go. I see Dean was here," I said.

"Yes, he loves working with Dean. Justin was so excited waiting for you to come, right, Justin? We were practicing and practicing." Mary prattled on as she adjusted Justin's body to ensure maximum comfort. The machine beeped again. "Don't forget to breathe, honey. He gets so excited when you come to teach him," Mary said. "I'll let you get to it. Let me know if you need anything." She walked out. Two days a week, from 5:00 to 7:30 p.m., I worked with Justin in his home. Justin had completed high school the year before but was eligible for services until the age of twenty-two. Because he was non-verbal, we worked on different ways to communicate using his eyes, vocalization, body movements, and assistive technology equipment.

"Okay, Justin, let's do our visualization and grounding techniques meditation video." I walked over and turned off the lights, turned on the small projection ball of light that put different colors on the ceiling, and started the video. The sounds of birds and tinkling music filled the air, and I held Justin's hand. We were connected. He was in there, and I felt him sigh in peace. "Close your eyes and make yourself comfortable. Take a deep breath in through your nose and slowly and gently breathe out through your mouth," said the female voice with a lovely British accent. I modeled this for Justin. The room was quiet as we engaged in a sixteen-minute meditation where we visualized a magic treehouse. At fourteen minutes, Justin and I were calm. "You feel very peaceful and very relaxed in your treehouse. Know that your treehouse is always here for you. In your treehouse, you are always safe, you are always loved." Justin and I looked at each other. "Are you ready for some music, Justin?" I turned off the meditation and started a song so we could move into our trials.

"What Makes You Beautiful" by One Direction played as I readied Justin's switch-activated toys. Justin gurgled as I danced and sang along. "Dance with me, Justin," I sang. He moved his head from side to side sporadically as the music played. He moved his right arm up and down, and his left hand moved back and forth. His mouth opened wide in a huge smile. As the music played, I took the buttons off his leg bands and stopped the music so I could reprogram the buttons with different requests.

"I want a doggie," I said into the green button, recording a command. Justin immediately gurgled in anticipation when he heard the word doggie. Justin loved his activated pink poodle toy. I then placed the button on Justin's right leg. I grabbed the red button and spoke into it, recording, "I want bubbles." I put the button on Justin's left leg near his hand, which was curled into a claw.

"Are you ready, Justin, to request either bubbles or your doggie? Wait, I will be right back," I said. When I walked back into his room I heard, "I want a doggie." Then a second later, "I want a doggie." I laughed.

"I heard you, little dude. You want to play with the doggie. I hear ya," I said as I hooked the switch to the dog, got out my timer, and sat down, positioning myself by his bed and holding the switch out next to his right arm. "You ready? You have three minutes. Let's see if you can break your record," I said. Justin hit the switch again and activated the doggie that I had placed on his chest. He twisted his head back and forth, gurgling in pleasure. The dog made a high-pitched squeak and moved its plastic body back and forth on his chest each time. Justin may have been encased in a weak body, but his soul and spirit were strong.

Recently, Justin moved out of state, and I know he is well taken care of, but I miss him. I miss Justin's expressive eyes, gurgling laugh, and contagious smile. Students with moderate to severe disabilities deserve to live lives to their fullest potential. Justin's family made this happen, but many young beautiful souls are living in group homes being cared for by staff. In the Coachella Valley, Angel View runs homes for individuals who have moderate to severe disabilities.

Working with Justin enriched my life and taught me to treasure the present moment. Justin and I also learned to communicate in unique ways. We connected on a deep level. He taught me to find joy in the simple pleasures of life. Justin's family showed me how important it was for the entire family to support one another. I will always remember Justin as a strong, courageous young man who made this world a happier place for me and others with the power of his joyful spirit. I still use those meditation videos with kids during the yoga class I teach at the continuation school. They remind me to stay present and that we all can create a safe, magical world within our minds and spirits if we just breathe and imagine.

Academy Years

The Academy was the alternative setting for students who didn't fit in a typical school setting in grades K–12. Built in 1938, it was a small, online, blended-learning school that was located right behind our high school. This was a public school that provided an alternative educational path. The Academy's buildings used to be part of the high school. The Academy was housed in two long, rectangular buildings that housed twelve classrooms built in the Spanish mission design. One day, my principal, Wilson Worth asked me, "Do you want to work over at The Academy during your prep? We pay you your per diem. All you need to do is support some kids on IEPs." Every teacher in high school received a period to prepare their lessons and manage their caseload in special education. If the school "bought" my prep, it was a lot of money, one-fifth of my salary. Roma told me, "As a teacher, never turn down extra money." I said yes to this opportunity, and this decision transformed my life, bringing me more dear students and educator friends.

I could walk to The Academy in five minutes from my classroom. Molly Thorpe taught in one of their programs. It was for middle school students who had been suspended from their home school. A few students in her class had IEPs. Molly, who is retired now and still a close friend, was a veteran teacher and former school administrator. She ran her classroom in an efficient, tough, loving manner. She met kids where they were academically, emotionally, and behaviorally. She gave them a higher purpose, to improve the world. I learned so much from

Molly in the years I worked with her in the classroom. Plus, she was in the best physical shape of any teacher I had ever met.

A new teacher should surround themselves with the best teachers. It is like playing any sport; you grow when you play someone better than you. Molly was a master teacher and athlete. The kids in her class were considered behavioral issues who needed to be housed somewhere due to expulsions. Molly made it feel like a privilege to be in the program. The students read and wrote on topics related to becoming model citizens. For example, they did not just recite the pledge. They spent time analyzing the language and learning the history of it. Then, Molly would have them write their own pledges to themselves. Molly showed me that great teaching could reach any student.

Students also gave back to the community. They helped Molly put together goodie bags for runners in the many 5K runs she organized for the city. I recall the day that I walked in, and they were constructing tutus for one of the runs. Students were silent as they wove gauzy-colored fabric into a belt to create patterns. If they finished enough tutus, they could make one for themselves. Plus, all students in her class could run in the numerous 5Ks she put on and receive a medal for completion. Many students participated in these runs. It is how I started running.

Molly invited me to volunteer on a Saturday and then run; I was hooked just like the kids. It is addictive to complete a race even if you are the last one to cross the finish line. Running builds capacity and perseverance, attributes that help students get back on track in their education.

We also gave back to the community with our weekly outings. One of the most memorable activities was our Friday trips to the park and Del Taco. The park was two blocks from the school. My prep period was before lunch, so it worked out perfectly. We would take a walk and pass out peanut-butter-and-jelly sandwiches and shoes to people who were living in the park. Saige, one of the middle school students, loved to help others. She walked up to people and said in a customer service voice, "Good morning, we made peanut-butter-and-jelly sandwiches. Would you like one?" They always said yes to Saige as her chocolate eyes radiated with compassion. Then she would ask, "Do you need a new pair of shoes and socks?" Many times the person would nod and receive a pair of gently used shoes and a new pair of socks. After we did our community service, we would walk a couple more blocks to Del Taco. Molly bought each kid a bean burrito or taco as their Friday treat. People said these were the "bad kids," but with the right support, they became thoughtful, compassionate human beings. Molly's running program became more and more popular, and she decided to train a group of staff and kids to run the L.A. Marathon. Students (Miguel, Ezra, and Shawn) and staff (Lynn, Barry, me, and Molly) would meet every Saturday to do our long runs. We ran shorter distances during the week on our own, following the Molly Thorpe training program. Molly organized all the local 5K runs, so these were part of our program. We ran the Turkey Trot and the Santa Run.

In March of 2014, we ran the LA Marathon led by the ultra-fit Molly. She found a way to provide us with yellow shorts, and tank tops that were emblazoned with Marathon Runners on the front, as well as a hotel room the night before. Molly was a pro at finding sponsorships. Who knows, she may have even paid for some of the trip herself. Everyone finished. Some fast runners finished quickly. Lynn Yada, the elementary teacher, finished right after Molly in four hours. Others, like me, took six hours. Barry, the security guard, took nine hours. Molly waited at the finish line for him. The finish line was dark and deserted when he finished. We all gained confidence after we finished our first marathon. But some students, once they left Molly's program, struggled. I wish I would have stayed in contact with Ezra after he graduated high school. He had such potential.

In 2019, we went to Ezra's funeral. He graduated high school and fell in with the wrong crowd. I can't help but feel like the system failed him. His body was found in the open desert. He was eighteen years old. Ezra is not forgotten. Recently, someone was arrested and charged with his murder. Ezra's girlfriend had a baby boy months after he was killed. I know Ezra's parents will tell his son about his passion for running. I will always remember Ezra's smile as he ran in his yellow and white marathon tank top and short shorts. If I close my eyes, I can still see him crossing the finish line of a race, his arms extended in joy. Ezra's story serves as a reminder of how easily young people can be led astray. Ezra's spirit is alive in our hearts and memories.

Another marathon finisher, Miguel, was athletically gifted, competing in triathlons and other events during his time with Molly and throughout his high school years. He was also in special education. Miguel's slim build and natural energy made him a natural when running, swimming, or cycling. After leaving Molly's classroom, Miguel attended the comprehensive high school where I taught. Due to our running time together, Miguel and I never had any issues. Other teachers would send him to me when he got upset. We rarely talked about the incident but would just catch up on our athletic endeavors as we both enjoyed competing in triathlons. After we chatted, he would calmly go back to class. It still makes me smile to remember the day when Miguel wore his shiny finisher's medal to school after his first triathlon. It went well with his baggy Nike shorts. He walked a little taller and smiled a little wider showing off his dimples. When I saw him and pointed at the medal, he laughed and shrugged as if to say, "Yeah, I did it." Yet, with all that, I feel like I failed Miguel. I failed so many students by not getting to know them better by listening. This book is for every student I have ever taught. I'm sorry if I wasn't there for you. Today, I do my best to listen to your stories by slowing down, taking a deep breath in and out through my nose, and opening my ears and heart.

Miguel was convicted of grand theft auto two years after graduating high school in 2018. I hope he got out and put his life back together using the skills he learned from marathons and triathlons. Work hard. Keep going. Pain is not the enemy. Think positively. Molly said it best, "We thought we could save them. We lost a little piece of ourselves along with them."

Other students persevered, like Saige, who succeeded despite the odds. She went on to graduate, has a job, and is attending community college. She is thriving. I teach with the understanding that knowledge is never forgotten. Experiences matter. Education can change lives, but not always in the way we expect, given our narrow perspectives on time. It took a lot for me to change. The time the students spent in Molly's class was not wasted. I am sure their memories of those years sustain them throughout their lives.

The students and I were grateful to have Molly teach us. Molly is one of those gifted people who does everything well. She retired and recently hiked up Machu Picchu at age sixty-six. Molly's current hobby is decorating cookies. Her cookies are so lovely it's a shame to eat them, although they taste great too. She made me an Easter Bunny cookie that I'm going to use for a cake topper at a friend's baby shower. If there were a "Great Cookie Decorating" reality television show, Molly would win.

A position opened up at The Academy in my sixth year of teaching at the high school. Wilson Worth, our beloved principal, retired, and he was replaced by Rick Shop. The staff rebelled against the new authoritarian principal. I tried to stay out of it.

One day, I submitted a leave for a personal necessity day. Rick Shop denied it. I could have just called in sick, but I wasn't sick. It was personal, so I would not tell him why I needed a day off.

We got into a disagreement as I walked to The Academy. "If you don't tell me, I'm going to deny it. There are too many of these days being requested by staff," Rick Shop said in a parental voice.

"Go ahead and deny it. By the way, I have never requested one of these days in five years. Check my sick time. I rarely even call off sick," I said and walked away. It was time to go. Looking back, I needed a change. It was draining to manage extreme behaviors, and I was tired mentally and emotionally. For years, I had been striving to provide a safe space for kids who were struggling. If I could save them, maybe I could save myself. But teachers are not superheroes. Moving to a new position allowed me a class environment where there was daily peace. Some people might say I was reliving my childhood those years spent teaching students with emotional disturbances. But, those years were magical, and I will always treasure the students and fellow educators I worked with.

Teachers need leaders who support them and treat them as individuals. If educational leaders want teachers to treat kids with respect and dignity, they must give it to teachers in return. This is one reason why many teachers are leaving education. It's not the kids or the teaching; it's everything else. When I don't feel respected and valued by a leader, I find a new school or position. If you treat me poorly, you don't get to have me on your team. I know my worth.

So I transferred to The Academy, full time, as a resource specialist and supported students in special education. It was an amazing gig. I got to work with Molly, Lynn, and some other teachers. Molly and Lynn were special. They had the ability to make learning relevant, rigorous, and emotionally meaningful. Not all teachers can do that.

When I walked into some of the classrooms to support these kids, they were glued to the computer on the self-paced learning program Edgenuity. I do not agree with students *only* learning through an online curriculum. It can be part of the learning or even the curriculum, but there has to be conversations, engagement, and interaction with one another and the world for learning to cement.

I enjoyed my position as I was given a lovely office and admired the principal, Dr. Tree. He treated me as a peer and mentored me. I was working on getting an administrative credential, a second master's, and a doctorate. Dr. Tree was a former special education teacher and a leader who promoted positivity and harmony. Even when teachers struggled, he would coach them and offer them numerous opportunities to improve. I remember one day I asked him about what he looked for in a teacher.

"I look for a strong commitment to kids and an excellent work ethic. You can teach pedagogy, but it is hard for someone's personality to change," he said. I find this to be true. Teachers who love and want what is best for kids can struggle in their first few years of teaching as it is a lot to master. However, with a lot of work and persistence, teachers can learn to manage the behaviors in the classroom and teach using research-based practices. I do not know how to teach someone how to love kids.

I still worked with Molly but also got to know Lynn, the elementary teacher. Lynn was one of the hardest-working teachers I had ever met, and it showed. Her classroom ran smoothly, and kids were always engaged in rigorous, high-level learning.

"I only get them two days a week, so we need to make the learning count," said Lynn. I had the honor of co-teaching with her. She would send me her slides on the weekend, and I would study them to prepare for my time in her classroom. We bounced off one another effortlessly. The other elementary teacher's work ethic was the opposite. I asked Jane Shields if we could do some co-teaching.

"Well, I mostly work one-on-one with kids. Just pull the kids out one by one and help them. This will take some of the workload off me," she said. It felt like Jane was teaching just for the paycheck.

I preferred working with Lynn. Lynn was in it for the kids. She did a lot of project-based learning. Her kids engaged in research, experiments, and stretched their minds. I loved working at this school, but it was still symptomatic of the bias against special education students and teachers. Molly and Lynn were the only teachers who treated me as an equal member of the classroom. The rest of the teachers considered me support staff. In some classes, I was a highly overpaid para-educator. Yet, the kids made it worth it.

Aaron was a student I supported in Lynn Yada's class. He looked like a miniature Paul McCartney. He was smart but was on the autism spectrum, so he could be very stubborn about what he decided to study.

"Aaron, it's time to do some math with Ms. Jackie," Lynn said. "Please close the computer, as your train schedules will still be there when you get back."

Aaron and I went to my office because he was easily distracted when asked to do math. I had a train sticker for him if he finished his math. Aaron knew all the schedules for trains and the makes and models of each of them. He also loved Rock Hudson and Doris Day movies.

"Did you know, Ms. Jackie, that Rock Hudson and Doris Day starred in three movies together? They're *Pillow Talk*, *Lover Come Back*, and *Send Me No Flowers*." I looked at Aaron and smiled. "I know I've seen *Pillow Talk*. I will watch the other ones, Aaron. Let's do our math."

"How is your dog? Her name's Elizabeth Barrett Browning, right? I think she's cute," said Aaron as he picked up the dog photo on my desk.

"Aaron, if you finish this math, we can also take a walk outside," I said. "We can talk about trains or whatever else you want. Let's get five problems done." Aaron sighed and got to work. Each individual is unique. Rather than trying to force Aaron to conform to a standard learning approach, I did my best to incorporate his interests into his learning experience.

We loved to walk around the small campus. We would sit under a tree, and I would listen to him explain about trains and their schedules for ten minutes. Those were beautiful days. Incorporating incentives such as train stickers and walks improved Aaron's work. Those memories of building relationships make me smile, as does the knowledge that Aaron is doing well and will graduate high school in 2025. Dr. Tree left after only working at the district for four years. Not all of the teachers at the school wanted harmony and peace. Shame on them.

Paper Magic

I first worked with Brenda Gunderson, the school counselor, at The Academy. Dr. Tree introduced me to her on the first day I started.

"This is Brenda Gunderson. Brenda is our wordsmith. You two will get along just fine," Dr. Tree said. "She always has a 'Brenda-ism' when we are troubled."

"Well, Ms. Jackie, we are a reflection of those who love and guide us," Brenda said with a smile. She wore a turquoise shirt with the word "gratitude" spelled out in rhinestones. I loved her already.

Brenda's magic power was transforming paper into art. One day, as I walked out of a classroom, I saw Brenda, accompanied by about twenty students ranging from first grade to high school age. They were all adorning a tree with beautiful hand-drawn gratitude cards.

"Now, kids, it's important to cultivate an attitude of gratitude. We always have something to be grateful for in life. These cards will remind us that even in hard times, we can be grateful," Brenda said.

"They're so pretty. Won't they float away?" a short student with thickly plaited braids asked.

"Now, I thought of that. That's why we will make sure they won't come off for a long time, so we are using this twine to connect each one to a branch," Brenda said. I watched as the kids and Brenda attached the bedazzled, brightly colored cards onto the tree. I smiled, waved goodbye to Brenda and the students, and went to my home and hospital gig with Justin.

Brenda was a counselor at the Learning Academy and strived to build relationships through hands-on art activities and discussions. She was a master at designing art lessons in which students created highly intricate cards, exploding boxes, and decorated journals. The kids changed when they were with Brenda. Maybe it was her ability to be vulnerable, or perhaps the hands-on activities, but the kids quieted down, focused, and were willing to speak about their feelings with Brenda. She taught me a lot about how to listen and hear students so that they felt valued. Brenda shared her own struggles of not feeling good enough and worthy with the kids. She was from Montana and small-town wisdom poured out of her.

"My sister was the beauty queen of our high school. I never could measure up to her in that way, so I had to find my own way to be pretty. That's why I use a lot of glitter and rhinestones. Everything's better with a little sparkle and bling," Brenda said. Then she would have kids sit in a circle and share their hopes, dreams, and fears. They had her full attention. Many times they would talk about problems within their families. Brenda would listen until they were done. Then she would say, "Honor the family you are born into, but you are responsible for the one you make." In other words, your family might not be what you think it should be, but without them, you wouldn't be here, so thank them for that, but create the family you want to have. The kids would nod; they heard her and were heard. Brenda was present in a way I yearned to be. Her blond head nodded in acknowledgment of their shared humanity. Her voice was husky when she said, "Oh, sweetie, thank you for sharing." I do what Brenda did back then when a student spoke: I lean in with my whole body and soul. Brenda disliked students using technology and some students struggled with letting go of their phones.

She would remind them that no one needed a phone. "Kids, be careful what you 'believe' for the inside of that very word is the word, 'lie.' I know you think you need a phone, but you don't. The world won't stop spinning. I promise." This was a harder sell for kids. Brenda came from a time when people looked one another in the eye and listened. Despite this issue with cell phones, the kids enjoyed creating beautiful projects with their own hands. Most of the students were also students of color. Brenda was blond and blue eyed, and some students, at first, thought this was an issue. Ms. Brenda quickly put this issue to rest.

"My grandchildren are biracial, so please, let's not go there," she said.

I always participated in the activities with the kids. Mine were always slightly lopsided and messy. I did not grow up with crafting. No one had taught me how to create arts and crafts before. I was like a kid with Brenda. She supported me hand over hand some days since I was a leftie. One day Brenda came up to me.

"Jackie, I know you say you aren't good at art, but you are welcome to come over to my house this Saturday to do a project. Molly, Maria, and Lynn, and I meet once a month. We do a potluck and craft. We are doing hand-decorated Christmas tree top hats."

"I love Christmas. I'm there," I replied.

Brenda's house looked like Martha Stewart had come over and decorated the entire house. There was not one but two Christmas trees. Her front porch had a large standing sign that had JOY stenciled on it, hand-painted and decorated by Brenda. We all brought a dish to share. Molly brought her vegan nachos. Mary brought a tortilla salad. Lynn brought fruit. I brought chips and hummus. Brenda supplied the drinks and the beautiful ambiance. We were somewhat of a diverse group. Brenda and Molly were blond and blue-eyed. Mary and I were Mexican. Mary spoke Spanish. I did not. Lynn was Japanese. We were different ages and from different political backgrounds too. But what we had in common was our love of learning and teaching. That night I got to know Mary, who radiated positivity. She worked in the computer lab supporting students as a paraeducator. Some of the teaching staff sent kids into the lab without asking, taking advantage of her love for the kids. Mary would use her energy supporting the students.

Mary left her earthly form a few years ago, a sudden and unexpected grief we all walked through together. She had worked at the school for many years, so many students and staff were devastated when they heard she had passed on unexpectedly. Brenda helped us keep Mary's memory alive by planting trees in her name. Our "Sisters with Scissors" crafting group still meets every month. Brenda has a photo framed of us that we took on that first night long ago when we crafted our Christmas top hats. We are all holding them and smiling. Mary's smile is so alive in the photo, it wants to leap out of the frame.

Molly, Lynn, and Brenda are all retired now. Yet, they keep very busy. Molly still organizes 5K runs for the city. Lynn volunteers at her father's assisted living facility, doing crafts with the residents. Brenda fosters kittens for the local humane society. These women continue to teach and serve their communities as it is just who they are. They are givers. No, they are not perfect. They are still teachers; they just don't have a classroom of kids. They give their wisdom to the world now. Giving enriches the lives of the givers.

I am the only one still teaching. When I returned to teach at the continuation high school, Brenda agreed to volunteer in my classroom during my Wednesday elective period. Once a month in my classroom for two years, Brenda passed her love of paper magic on to a group of students. Students folded, hot glued, and bedazzled paper into creations only Brenda could have facilitated. She would spend countless hours creating these lessons. She would also use her own money to buy supplies. This is another issue in education: funding. It takes time and money to create beautiful crafts. Brenda had collected hundreds of supplies over her years of crafting, and she would donate them to our students. Sometimes I would try to pay her, and she would always say, "I get a lot out of working with the kids. It gives me purpose after retiring."

When the students finished the hour-and-a-half class, they always had something memorable to keep or to give to a loved one. Last year, we made heart-shaped Valentine's Day letter holders. I adorned mine with stickers with positive affirmations and gave it to my sister for her birthday. She put it up in her office.

Not every student enjoyed making these creations or giving up their cell phones for an hour and a half to connect with Brenda. But they did it. Some more willingly than others. Brenda always noticed when kids left their art projects with me, and I saw a slight dim in her smile for a moment. But then she would shake it off with a flick of her blond hair.

"Jackie, I admire you as it must seem impossible to get through to these kids. But if you divide the word, it says 'I'm possible.' Remember that when you work with these kiddos because some of them are interesting," Brenda said as I walked her to her car when the bell rang and lunch began.

Raul, one of our students, struggled with folding the papers in an intricate manner. I did too, so I was no help. Brenda sat with Raul and showed him step by step the order of the folds needed to create the intricate box. He added his stickers and hot-glued the rhinestones.

"I'm giving this to my mom," Raul said.

Astoria, who was slight of frame, with pink hair, and a style all her own, always wore a face mask. She was a natural at folding, gluing, and layering the paper to create intricate designs. Astoria loved a bird motif, and Brenda made sure to bring her plenty of avian stickers. Astoria was typically quiet in class, but when Brenda was there, she would brighten and giggle, answering Brenda's questions in a soft voice. Raul and Astoria have both graduated, but they have magical paper creations to remember their time with Brenda. Brenda is now fostering kittens so she will not be volunteering this current school year. She gifted me a sound bowl this summer to carry on the positive energy she helped create within the walls of our classroom.

One of the significant challenges facing teachers is financial strain. Despite our crucial role, we often face inadequate compensation. Many educators, myself included, dip into our own pockets to purchase classroom supplies, educational materials, and even basic necessities for our students. I have spent thousands of dollars over the course of my teaching career. I have always worked extra duty as a teacher. Right now, I work Wednesday evenings as an adjunct professor for a teacher preparation program. I also coach softball, am the equity lead, and work on some Saturdays presenting on unconscious bias. I still have a high student loan payment each month too. But, I continue to spend money to provide snacks to my students, buy birthday cards and incentives, and supplies for special projects. I am committed to doing my best to provide a well-rounded education for students. But, I do question a system that makes it necessary for teachers to use their salary to fund education.

Burned Out

Even with the change of schools I was ready to move in a new direction in the education field. It took me twenty years to finally burn out. Working fulltime as a teacher while pursuing my doctoral degree didn't help. Special educators are especially vulnerable to burnout, due to many factors including the unique demands of managing diverse learning needs and navigating complex individualized education plans (Emery & Vandenberg, 2010; Y. L. Lee et al., 2011).

During my time at the academy, I was asked to coach new or struggling teachers part-time after school. I had a hard time saying no to any opportunity. Since I was young, I was always trying to be good enough. Now I know I'm good enough. My sponsor in sobriety always reminded me, "Jackie, you don't have to do anything or become anything to be loved. You're loved by God for being born." Back then, I was still trying to prove myself worthy. Worthy of love, worthy of the gift of teaching, and worthy despite my past. I thought that if I got the highest degree or position, then I would be happy. Now I know it is not about the exterior of life. It is an inside job. So, I was convinced it was time to move up in the school system. My mindset was all wrong. I admit it. I thought I could change the world more as a coach or possibly as an administrator. I was wrong.

After a couple of years, a full-time position as a coach for special education teachers opened up, and I interviewed for and secured the position. I worked under the director of human resources, Dr. Elegent, who was a humane and positive leader. I enjoyed coaching new teachers on how to be their best teaching selves and collaborating with veteran teachers to enhance their practices. Coaching felt like a natural fit for me. I honed my presentation skills as we conducted monthly sessions for new special education teachers. Dean Troup, my friend, was also hired as a coach. The training sessions we led, including one where we blindfolded staff members and had them decorate a cake together, were unforgettable.

As a full-time coach, I observed many classrooms and teachers. It was a point in my life that opened my eyes to the challenges in our schools. Many new teachers struggled with classroom management. It took years, but I transitioned from an authoritarian-style teacher to one who prioritized kindness and love. However, I recognized that a robust classroom management system was essential for effective learning. Teaching with courage and love meant ensuring students understood expectations and were held accountable. This proved to be a challenge for new teachers, who often just wanted to teach. Weren't they hired to teach the curriculum? But without establishing relationships with students and setting clear agreements within the classroom, disruptive behavior would ensue. I realized even more the importance of getting to know students before attempting to teach them.

Many issues stem from our theoretical teacher education programs. Teachers are instructed in theoretical solutions to classroom management problems and are often taught to exert control. Some new teachers attempt to control everything in their classrooms, leading to student rebellion and disruptive behavior. Others aim to befriend their students. Neither approach alone is effective. Effective teaching requires time to develop a balanced approach to classroom management that suits both the teacher and the students. This is an aspect teaching programs don't often emphasize; becoming a proficient teacher takes time. You will make mistakes! That's part of the process. The first-year path of a teacher involves learning the curriculum, understanding the students, and self-reflection.

During this time, I completed a second master's, an administrative credential, and a doctorate. My doctoral research focused on teachers' perceptions of student engagement and behavior following activity bursts in the classroom. In December of 2018, I became Dr. Mantz—a moment that profoundly impacted me. No one can take away your education. But I still was not satisfied. Maybe if I moved to an administrator position, I would be satisfied?

Despite my love for coaching, I decided to pursue administrative positions within the district. Had I written this book two years ago, I would have shared a different story about why being an administrator didn't work out for me. I've chronicled those experiences elsewhere, but what's important to clarify before delving into these two years is that administration was never my calling. It took prayer, meditation, writing, therapy, and time to come to this realization. I wrote the next story a few months after I stepped down from my position as a program specialist for the school district where I still work in the Coachella Valley. I was devastated by what I perceived as my failure as an administrator. It took me years to see that God was doing for me what I could not do for myself. I have faith in "Good Orderly Direction," in a higher power, and in love. If I had not had such a negative experience as an administrator, I may have continued on that journey.

Working as an administrator reminded me of the life I didn't want to live. I needed to fulfill my life's purpose: to teach. I now know precisely what I want to do for the remaining years of my life on this planet. And for that clarity, I am deeply grateful.

Administrative Hell

When I became an administrator at the district office in special education, I thought I had made it. I had a posh, albeit shared, office in our gleaming brand-new building. The colors of the carpet (orange and green) even matched my own mid-century modern vibe. After the first week, I knew I had made a mistake. I realized as the hours turned to days and days turned into months that I did not fit in this job. I felt like my chubby childhood self, trying to fit into those Calvin Klein jeans Brooke Shields wore, but I couldn't even get them past my hips.

People called my position the most stressful job in the district. A former assistant director of special education said to me in jest, "Program specialists either have a heart attack, go out on stress leave, or find a new job." She left our district soon after. What made it almost even worse is that I loved education. My years of teaching were some of my best firsts, such as the first day of school. I treasure the memory of the first time I read a student's writing where they bared their soul with such courage, not knowing yet how to sound less like themselves. Teaching never, and I mean never, was my worst job, as there were always those students that made it worth it all.

As a special education administrator, I felt like I was in *The Matrix*. There were students who needed resources and support from the district. Yet the educational machine forced me to uphold the status quo, and IEP meetings were adversarial. The district had one vision for the stakeholders and another for the students. There was no Neo or Morpheus to help me get out of the maze I found myself in day after day. So maybe that's why, one night, a few years ago, I yelled to the hummingbirds in my backyard, "FUCK THIS SHIT!" Lizzy and Sparrow, my Boston Terriers, cocked their heads as if to ask, "What next?"

Have you ever had that moment in your life where everything becomes crystallized in your mind's eye? I had that moment, and my mind was clear. I knew I had to make a decision after the final incident with the special education director. I realized she was not the problem. It was the "matrix" of special education that was the problem. I could continue to work in a system that I could no longer tolerate or accept, or I could resign and go back to teaching where things made sense.

I knew that if I put all this energy, every piece of my heart and soul into my classroom, my students would respond. They always did; students learn from someone they care about and who cares about them. My last day as an administrator was June 24th, 2021. Now I teach core classes at a continuation high school in the Coachella Valley. The worst job ever was actually the best thing that could have happened to me. Now I know exactly where I fit. I am a teacher.

Just One Story

Memory is a strange thing. One night I was reminded of why I made the right decision to step down from my program specialist position in special education. I had a dream that I was still working in the department, and it left me shaking and filled with dread upon awakening. In the dream, I was in an IEP meeting with twenty people. There were lawyers for both the district and the parent. I was navigating the avoidance of a possible lawsuit. My knees were shaking under the table, and I couldn't breathe. Then I awoke. I realized that was the reason that administration is not for me. I am too empathetic, and I can't deal with such toxicity. But now, I'm at home, safe.

Mr. Pickle

One day, while I was still a program specialist, the other program specialist, Marcia, walked into my office. I was sitting at my desk reviewing a report. I clicked off my screen and turned around when I heard Marcia's voice, in that high octave she only displayed when things were unbelievable.

"Jackie, you won't believe this one."

"It's the special ed dept, I'll believe anything."

"Today I went into Minnie's office to have a courageous conversation with her. Instead, she stopped me in mid-speech and said, 'I know exactly what you need.' Minnie then brought out a plush stuffed pickle from her drawer and said, 'Let's dress Mr. Pickle.' She then pulled out a purple miniature dress from her drawer and slid the dress carefully over the plush pickle's form."

"What did you do?"

"Nothing. I was dumbfounded by Mr. Pickle in the purple dress." Marcia continued, "This is why people think our department is bat-shit crazy. Do you know the other day I walked in, and Cindy and Minnie were running around the office launching rubber chickens at one another? Then they launched the chickens at staff members. It was just weird. Other people from different departments walked by and just stared."

As I walked to my car, I saw Marcia walking to her car. We stopped and looked at one another. I started laughing. Marcia's laughter echoed mine. I stopped and held my stomach as people walked past me, filing out at the end of the day.

I miss Marcia. She could have been the director. She had a photographic memory of education code, was disciplined and hard-working, and understood people. Marcia was passed over for a promotion and left to go to a nearby district soon after. Instead, we had this woman "leading" our department who went from one extreme to another. One day she was dressing Mr. Pickle. The next she was making snap decisions which we had to reel from and do our best to recover after the shrapnel hit us from all sides. The special education department was a mess, but they had done me a favor. If it hadn't been such a toxic environment, I might have stayed. I might have stayed if I was not told during staff meetings to not speak of the issues facing the classrooms I visited. I could not, would not, live a life of silence.

In my term as an administrator, I realized there was so much darkness in the world. I felt like the darkness was overwhelming me some days. This was during the time when George Floyd was murdered. I didn't know what to do, but I had to do something. So I decided to volunteer for the Prison Education Project (PEP). One of the classes I could teach was autobiographical writing. I would work one-on-one with a woman currently incarcerated who wanted to write about her life. I would also write about my life as an example. This would be done via email or back then JPay. I never thought teaching a student like Tessa, someone I would come to know and work with, would lead us to writing and publishing our stories. These are the promises of sobriety revealed.

Prison Education Project

Volunteering with PEP was the answer for me. It is the largest volunteer-based organization in the United States, committed to expanding educational opportunities for the in-custody population. When I volunteered for PEP and signed up to facilitate the Introduction to Autobiography class, I had no inkling that this was the beginning of a beautiful journey with a fellow writer. Tessa, the first student I worked with at PEP, is incarcerated at a prison in California. As a longtime teacher, I knew how to build trust with students in person. How could I build trust with Tessa via email? When I wrote to Tessa, I was nervous. It was 6 a.m. on a Friday. We were only allowed to write on Fridays per the prison's guidelines. I wrote, "Assignment 1 Autobiography: Write a 1-page Biography; Why is your life's story compelling? Why is it unique? Greetings Tessa, this is Jackie, I will be your new writing instructor facilitating the writing of your story. I look forward to working with you to write your story. I am so honored to be able to hear your story. I hope you are well and you find joy somehow even through these times."

Tessa wrote me back and responded to the writing prompt. We wrote to one another, responding to the prompts, for seven weeks. As I read her story, I felt deep within that God's providence was somehow to be found in it all. We were both souls in search of forgiveness and on a path to finding the light and love within. Our book was written during the time of the pandemic shutdown. Before we wrote our chapters, we engaged in written small talk. I shared stories about my dogs. She shared what it was like within stone walls. On Dec. 3rd, 2020, she wrote:

> "I have been helping in the unit a lot because the regular volunteers got quarantined, plus I took over decorating the unit for Christmas... We're on lockdown (which is fine by me! I get more done!). We're supposed to get off lockdown on the 10th, but I'm sure they'll put us back on around Christmas until after the new year."

We connected by sharing our everyday lives. But I was riveted by the words of her life story. Friday morning at 6 a.m., I read her first words:

> Although I've never met him, I've been haunted by my brother my entire life. He's always managed to show up somehow, even before I knew he existed. Sometimes he'd come in the guise of a friend who was "like a brother to me." Other times he'd appear in my dreams. When I was a young child playing make-believe games, I'd almost always pretend to be a boy. As an adult, I would come to understand that I was pretending to be him (Tessa McCarty, *Embracing Dawn*).

I saw multiple connections within our lives. Tessa's writing was vivid, and I knew others had to read our stories. One year later, we published our book with the help of PEP. Both of us used pen names. I published under 'Marie Rodriguez.' Tessa used a pen name too. PEP provided an editor and even gave each of us printed copies of our books. All proceeds from the book were donated to a victim's scholarship fund and PEP. Writing my story and reading Tessa's story freed something in me. I let go of the shame of my past.

Tessa was barely an adult when she committed murder. She was given a long sentence. (I am being deliberately vague since

Tessa's story is hers to tell, not mine.) As for me, I was a teenager when I almost died from overdosing on alcohol.

> "I remember going into convulsions and throwing up vodka. I remember the feel of the cement on my knees as I bent over and spewed vodka out of my nostrils and mouth." (Marie Rodriguez, *Embracing Dawn*).

Tessa and I had so much in common. I struggled until I was twenty-four, when I began to turn my life around. Then I found teaching, which gave me a reason to stay sober and care for others. Incarcerated, Tessa found sobriety and a connection to God. She wrote:

> My heart stopped when I heard the date. I couldn't believe it. I felt my face get pale, but Angie and Chap were too busy talking about the baptism to notice. The sound of their conversation faded as I drifted into my thoughts. The date that Chap had picked had special significance to me. Six years prior, on that exact day, I had made the worst decision of my life. So many lives had been torn apart by my selfishness that day, and I would give anything to be able to go back and undo it. But I knew I would never be able to take it back. I had spent every anniversary of that day entrenched in a deep pit of self-loathing and depression, and now Chap had picked that very day. My stomach sank as I realized that I was going to be baptized on the anniversary of the day I had committed my crime (Tessa McCarty, *Embracing Dawn*).

As I transcribed our book, I knew we had done something worthwhile. Looking back, I am amazed at how much trust and faith we gave one another. I am so grateful for Tessa and her courage to tell her story. The experience changed me forever as I discovered my authentic self by writing my story with another woman.

I asked Tessa to reflect on her journey. She wrote:

> As time goes on, I feel more and more grateful to PEP for giving me such a wonderful opportunity. I am still amazed by all the hard work that my writing partner, Jackie (Marie), and I put into it. What's more, is that so many people have come forward to share how our writing has touched them. I am so humbled by the fact that Jackie and I were able to use our journeys and struggles to help others. I now know that I can accomplish anything I set my mind to, and can now embrace my past with love (Tessa McCarty, *Embracing Dawn*).

I hope to see Tessa in person someday. We lived for a year writing pages of memories. We could not live the rest of our lives here. We had to move forward to a warm, forgiving place of sand rather than stone. But we are bound by our journey from stone to sand, forever.

Following my collaboration with Tessa, I continued volunteering to help other women write their stories through classes with PEP for another year. Volunteering with PEP also led me to the unique experience of teaching in Africa via Zoom.

Are We Together?

"I look deep into the lion's eyes. It was me or him, so I stab him with my spear. Chack, chack, chack, whumpf, whumpf," said the writer as he grasped an imaginary spear. He puffed out his cheeks to make the sound of the spear hitting the lion's flesh. Helin, Los, and I were open-mouthed as we listened to our fellow writers. They sat together in white plastic chairs with their journals and pencils in hand, telling their stories via Zoom in our final creative writing class.

There are times when one feels compelled to do something. For years, I dreamed of teaching in prisons. I could have easily been in prison if I had not gotten sober and found teaching. I thought, "There but for the grace of God go I."

Two other writers taught the class with me. Helin was a working writer, and Los was a poet who had just finished law school. The course was held online via Zoom as the writers were incarcerated in Luzira Maximum Security Prison in Uganda, Africa. Luzira Maximum Security Prison houses both men and women. It is the only maximum-security prison in the country. According to the Human Rights Reports by the Department of Justice in 2020, there are human rights issues involving citizens who are arbitrarily arrested or detained in Uganda. There are also political prisoners in Luzira. Some prisoners spend years in prison awaiting trial only to have the court find insufficient evidence to justify their detention.

The all-male class of students was dressed in bright orange and yellow smocks. The one guard in the room was always friendly and helpful. He stood to the side in his green uniform and beret. We taught the class at 8 p.m. on Sundays. Across the world in Uganda, it was 10 a.m. on Monday morning. The classes lasted an hour and a half.

At the beginning of the first class, students introduced themselves. "Greetings gentlemen. Are we together?" I asked as I put my hands into the shape of a circle. Everyone put their hands into a circle and held it up to their chests. This was a cultural reference from the country taught to us by PEP, and we used it to connect. "Name a place where you would like to set a creative writing piece. Share out your name and the setting of your writing piece," I said after Helin, Los, and I introduced ourselves and welcomed the writers to class. There were around fifteen men in the room, and they all took turns introducing themselves and their story settings. Most of the men set their stories in their villages in Africa or in prison. Many wrote of their struggles before their time in prison. They wrote of struggling to eat and searching for work in the cities. Others wrote of love lost and betrayal. Their stories flowed, naturally embedded with figurative language and metaphor. The Zoom connection went in and out, so we had to keep waiting for them to log back on. By the end of the hour-and-a-half class, we had learned all the writers' names and something about their stories.

During the second class, we discussed origin stories. "We always want to know our character's backstory. An example of this is a superhero's origin story," said Los. The creative writing class morphed into a writing workshop where the writers responded to prompts and shared their writings. Most of the classes were spent listening and offering bits of input on the use of dialogue and imagery.

This is how the last few classes would typically go. Helin, Los, or I (we mixed it up) would ask students to share their writings from the homework the week before. Numerous hands would pop up, and we would smile and laugh together. We would let each writer read their stories or poems for three to five minutes. After they finished, we would state what we noticed and ask questions. The writer would furiously write down the notes and thank us with a nod of his head with his hands clasped together. We would get to as many people as possible and then start again the next week. It was hard to stay within the time limit.

These men were bursting with stories, with tales they needed to write and speak to the world. During these moments spent online, I felt like I was overseas sitting in a room with writers in Africa, not at my computer in Cathedral City. The reality was these men were incarcerated. Some were facing the death penalty or life in prison. Their society may have put them behind stone walls, but their voices were strong, vibrant, and alive.

At the next class, Helin asked, "Who wants to come up? Don't be shy."

"I will read mine," said Ali. He had a shaved head and dimples. His smile was as bright as his yellow smock and pants. We all sat and waited as he walked up to the screen.

"This goes out to Queen Jackie. It is a letter of hope and love from across the seas." How I wish I had the letter to me as it combined Ali's love for America and boxing with his crush on me. We snapped when it was done, and I tried not to blush.

"Thank you, Ali. Interestingly, I write to people I admire all the time," I said.

"Do they write you back?" asked Ali.

"Yes, my favorite author, Mary Doria Russell, wrote me back. Read *The Sparrow*, gentlemen, if you can get a copy," I said. They all nodded and wrote the name of the book down.

Helin and Los called me "Queen Jackie" in jest for the rest of the class. Names were important. PEP encouraged all teachers to use the writers' names as much as possible during classes so they would feel seen and heard. It worked. We were all connected, a circle of writers sharing our stories with one another. One of the ways we were able to connect with the students was by sharing our own stories. Helin, Los, and I were all authentic, speaking of our lives and struggles. I discussed my sobriety and the grace it gave me to write. Some writers nodded, and I recognized kindred souls. Los discussed poetry with the writers and told them about his favorite poet, a Portuguese man named Fernando Pessoa, who had written poetry under at least eighty-one names. Helin brought her cat Khaki up to the screen, and he became the official mascot of the class. The men always asked about Khaki.

"Say hi to Khaki. Tell him we miss him," the gentlemen would say right before we logged off. In our last class, all the writers read a piece of their writings. Many of the gentlemen sang songs to us or quoted biblical scripture, wishing us health and peace. At 10 p.m., the guard said we had to log off. We did not want to go. The hope in the room was intoxicating. We could all feel it and wanted to hold onto it as long as possible.

"We hope you come to Africa to teach us in person. We will be waiting," said a young man who looked all of sixteen years old. PEP succeeds in working within prisons because it operates within the system. PEP works with correctional facilities in a collaborative manner and follows the rules and policies within the institution, without questioning or challenging them. Yet it was still troubling to see these redeemable men behind prison walls. My dream is to someday journey to Uganda, meet my fellow writers, and hear their stories face to face.

The Light in Me Bows to the Light in You

During my time at PEP, my friend Chanel and I taught a yoga and meditation class via Zoom at a medium-security county juvenile detention center in Riverside, California. This facility houses forty-four juvenile males. They are among the nearly sixty thousand incarcerated individuals under age eighteen in the U.S.

During the seven-week yoga class, we met two young men who will remain forever in my mind's eye. Mario, who attended from weeks one through five, was doing push-ups on his light blue mat and clapping his hands together when we logged on. He was full of energy but settled down when we began breathing in through our noses and out through our mouths. Yoga is not simply a workout. Yoga is a philosophy that can teach people how to live life in a positive manner. Every week we would review a portion of the eight limbs of yoga, move into asanas (poses), and finish with a meditation exercise.

"Are you going to show us some harder poses this time?" Mario asked when we returned for the second session. "I really liked doing this yoga stuff." The yoga philosophy apparently resonated with him. "Ya know, I might use this yoga and meditation stuff with my girl as we kinda have a toxic relationship," he said matter-of-factly. Our class felt like a home of stretching, peace, and breath where we honored the light in one another.

In the fifth week of class, Mario was gone. One of our new students, Tony, paid rapt attention as we reviewed the basics of yoga and meditation. As we finished with a visualization meditation on finding one's happy place, Tony bowed his head and said reverently, "Namaste, I appreciate you both, and I'll be back next week. I get out soon, and I want to learn as much as I can so I can be there for my daughter." Chanel summed up our class with these words she wrote to me recently:

"Jackie and I were able to teach lessons of gratitude, mindfulness, and the importance of daily movement. These weekly lessons created an opportunity for our students to learn and give themselves self-care, peace, and love. We showed our students that they themselves and no one else are in control of their happiness and their outlook on life. The students opened their hearts up to us, showed us their inner light, and honored the light within Jackie and me. They actively practiced the concept of 'Namaste.' For this reason, and many others, leading this course with Jackie has been one of the most fulfilling experiences of my life."

Teaching yoga with PEP inspired me to become yoga certified through the Breathe for Change yoga school and then receive an additional certification through Kootenay Yoga School. This led me to be able to eventually teach an elective P.E. yoga class at the continuation school where I am currently teaching. Everything is connected. Like my friend Stan in sobriety says, "There is no bad or good, just opportunities to learn something."

I took a step back from PEP to focus on writing this book. But recently, I attended the training session needed to resume my volunteer work with them. In a few weeks, I will teach a course on college success on Saturdays within stone walls. I made the decision, after speaking with my husband Joe, to teach in-person within a women's prison. I am ready.

Continuation School Years

When I stepped down from my position as a program specialist, I asked to be put in a general education position. Teachers, always give yourself options. I rarely used my general education credential, but now it was a lifeline. If I did not have a general education credential, I would have left teaching. When I had my exit interview with Minnie, the director of special education, I told her, "I would rather Uber than teach in the special education department. Human resources already agreed to put me in a general education position. I will not work for you ever again." It was my *Jerry Maguire* moment. Minnie was eventually fired last year. It took me a long time to forgive her and wish her well. But, I realize she had given me the greatest gift: I teach.

I was first offered a position teaching English at a comprehensive high school. I accepted the position. Then, providence once again laid its hand upon mine, and I saw an inter-district transfer posting within our district to teach English at a continuation high school. It was just down the street from the comprehensive high school. When I interviewed with David Houser, the principal, I felt comfortable. We just talked. I spoke of how I loved to teach writing. We also spoke of my work with the Prison Education Project.

"I won't ask you questions about flexibility and differentiation as I know as a special education teacher, you did this with students," David said with a smile. David looked like the poster boy for principals. He was tall, slim, blond, and had blue eyes that were kind. He hired me. The first day I walked into our classroom a week before school began, I rubbed my hands together and got to work. Instead of paper on the walls, I hung cloth. One was a thin, lime green carpet spun in Morocco. Another cloth wall hanging had a mandala on it, and yet another had a picture of a tree on it. I collected yoga mats and put them out (This would foreshadow me getting to teach yoga at the continuation school) for flexible seating. I bought three diffusers and essential oils.

Why? Students spend an epic amount of their lives in classrooms across the country. We all need to feel safe in our classes, our schools, and our hallowed halls of learning. So extra pencils and pens were on a table, water was available, and there were snacks for hungry kids and the teacher. The first day of school, I said, "Mi clase es tu clase." I continue to say this when kids ask for a tissue, to wash their hands, or just need a safe space.

This is one way I created a "stamily." This word, on the wall of our classroom, was created with a series of gold embossed gratitude cards. In 2021, the students and I came up with this definition. A "stamily" is defined as a classroom community where we all have the stamina and support to succeed and flourish. This includes the teacher as well as the students. We are all connected. The foundation of our home was set up, but that was merely the beginning. After being in classrooms as a teacher, a teacher's coach, and an administrator, I felt there was a lack of connection, relationships, and authenticity in teaching. My goal was to listen rather than talk, communicate rather than nag or berate, and expect the unexpected out of students.

We started the year off by writing letters, doing vision boards, and reading *The Four Agreements* by Don Miguel Ruiz. We still read it every first quarter to cement the agreements into our culture. Students would write about how the agreements related to their own lives. Their writings and stories awakened something deep and primitive. I wanted these students to thrive, not just survive. They had stories of overcoming struggles I had never known. They were only teenagers but had lived through a lot. I let go of an authoritative attitude, for the most part. Students got to hear some of my story. I was sober, had almost dropped out of high school, and lived with anxiety. It wasn't as if I just dumped all my personal stuff on these kids, nope. But, I told real stories about life. It is not an understatement to say students at our schools have struggled. They were just coming back from Covid when I returned to the classroom. The socioeconomic area is a challenge. There are gangs, drug and alcohol use, and trauma. This does not define our students or families. They have so many strengths, so I choose to see their assets rather than their deficits. Many students help care for their siblings, work, and go to school. This work ethic will carry them far in life, be it to college, university, trade school, or a job. "There are many ways to get to Texas," said my former principal, Wilson Worth. He was right. Success needs to be redefined within the educational system. For me, I am a successful teacher if students learn to read critically, use their voices powerfully in their writings, and become better humans. I can sleep at night if this happens on a daily basis.

One difference in teaching I found this time around was that I spent a lot more time planning. This was due to a renewed sense of purpose, but I also had much more time as I was now a general education teacher. No more IEPs to distract me from teaching. As a general education teacher, I never have to sacrifice my students' educational opportunities to do paperwork. This is not a diatribe or a rant against special education. I love all kids, and all kids deserve the best education. Now that I am in the general education field, I have my entire prep period to prepare. Special education teachers spend their entire preps doing paperwork. How is this equitable for kids? There have been recent improvements in this area. Special education teachers in my district were finally given two prep periods a day, acknowledging they are doing two jobs in one: teaching students and managing a caseload of IEPs.

Truth or Dare Rant

Yesterday, Tupac sang to us of crack sold to kids on the streets.

Some nights, can't get no sleep as I drug kids with fake morality hiding the inequity with peppermint Red Bird HANDCRAFTED CANDY.

Chew on them too so the hunger to wake kids up with truth lessens.

Lies echo in our multi-purpose room as kids say, "This isn't food," as they tear their Taco Nadas out of the plastic wrappers, guzzle grape juice, still hungry, no seconds and seconds to the bell.

Someone else's artificial truth lies in the history books doing my best like Don Miguel Ruiz says to do but it's not good enough.

Must stay on the units of study where somehow in a room filled with white male history teachers.

Mayan, Aztec, and Incas were ignored, forgotten.

These moments define so forget the damn, whatever, I'm queen of this class, emboldened by Nespresso coffee, we turn to page 128.

Back-to-School Night

Back-to-School Night is a yearly event for teachers, students, and guardians throughout the United States. It is held in the evening, lasting a couple of hours, during which teachers prepare their rooms with classwork and welcome families. I use the term "guardian" to encompass grandparents, other family members, and foster parents raising our students. I teach high school. Typically, Back-to-School Night is not well attended. I enticed my students with offers of sweets and extra credit.

Nine parents showed up. They signed in and walked around our classroom, with the students mostly accompanying them. I learned a lot. One mother informed me that two siblings were actually twins. Twins? How did I not know that already? A quiet male student lit up when his grandparents visited, talking more than he ever had in my class. Another student's dad nodded at his son as we talked, and the son nodded back in respect. Now I knew who to call. Parents' faces brightened when students showed them their work on the wall, and I mentioned how well they were doing in class. Here are a few statements I heard that first Back-to-School Night:

One parent said, "I'm so glad to hear it, as she had such a hard time at her last school during virtual learning. She's been through a lot, so I'm glad she's doing well. Call me if there's even an issue."

"They need to feel accepted and safe in class," a mom said while the student sat behind a mask silently. I listened and gave the guardians a letter I had written for them. As they walked out, guardians and students dropped a gratitude card into a glass jar. Here is a copy of the letter I wrote to them.

Good Evening,

Thank you for attending Back-to-School Night. Your time is valuable, and I appreciate you visiting our classroom. My name is Jackie, and with our students, I go by Dr. Mantz. I am proud and honored to teach your child this year. My first step as a teacher this year was to promote a healing, positive classroom, so we started many classes with quiet breathing exercises. In terms of education, I teach English and history. In both classes, we read a lot and discuss what we read. Additionally, we engage in projects and lots of writing. My goal is to help our students develop their critical thinking and comprehension skills, become avid readers, and learn to use writing as a powerful tool for good in the world.

My grading system is pretty simple. I try to give them as many opportunities to succeed as possible. Basically, all work is done in class, so they need to come to school and do the work.

Please help me. Let's ensure they have good attendance. They can make up any work they miss. If you need anything, please do not hesitate to call me on my Google Voice. I believe in your child. They have so much potential. Thanks again for coming to our class. Please fill out a gratitude card before you leave and drop it in the jar. I am grateful you came tonight.

Respectfully,

Dr. Jackie Mantz

I wish more parents would come to Back-to-School Night, but I understand that many families have other obligations. So, I sent a letter home with every student, along with my Google Voice number attached. Then, I called every student's home just to say hello and share one good thing about their child.

Many parents only spoke Spanish. The struggle of not knowing Spanish is real. Not understanding or speaking Spanish stopped me as a child from communicating with my grandfather, and it continues to impede my communication with students' families. However, I utilize paraeducators, office staff, and Google Translator in emergencies. Here is one more story, in third-person perspective, from my childhood, dealing with the language barrier.

Abuelo and the Shiny Coins

Jackie, Juanita, and Annie playfully pinched each other as their mom pulled up the dirt road in their brown Pinto station wagon. Jackie and Juanita were dressed alike in jeans and T-shirts as usual, but it wasn't hard to tell the twins apart. Juanita was skinnier than Jackie; everyone called Jackie "the chubby twin." Annie was dressed in a pink dress and sandals. Her straight black hair shone as she had brushed it over and over. Jackie and Juanita pulled each other's curly, messy hair and stuck out their tongues at Annie, who always looked like she had stepped out of a baby doll magazine. They piled out, running up the driveway into their abuelo's arms. Their abuelo lived in Corona, California, about a forty-five-minute drive from their home in Ontario. The smell of manure permeated the air.

"It stinks like poop," whispered Jackie. They all giggled. Juanita elbowed her identical twin and little sister. She was the oldest, and it was up to her to keep them in line. Abuelo lived alone, but their mom visited him every weekend. She would do his laundry, bring him groceries, and spend time with him. Sometimes, their mom would cook him Mexican rice and ground beef tacos, the only dishes she could cook well enough for him to enjoy. Tonight she had splurged and brought Pioneer Chicken to him in the red bucket. The girls' mouths were already watering in anticipation of the crunchy, flavorful skin.

"When do we get to eat?" Jackie asked loudly. Her mom threw her a hush-your-mouth look.

"Buenos días, nietas, me han hecho falta toda la semana," he said.

"Hey, Pop," said their mom.

The three girls didn't understand his words, but they felt the warmth of their Abuelo's hug.

"Abuelo said he missed you girls," their mom explained.

"Love you, Abuelo," they said.

"Say te amo Abuelo," their mom instructed.

"Te amo Abuelo," Juanita, Jackie, and Annie sang as they held their hands out like when they went to receive Holy Communion, and shiny coins spilled into their hands. Their mom and Abuelo waved them off as they spoke in rapid-fire Spanish. She started washing his dishes as soon as the girls left for the store.

The girls walked down the dirt road to Rodriguez Market. It looked like a farmhouse with its red and white paint. They pushed the door, which tinkled as they entered. They stuck candy into the paper bags Mr. Rodriguez had given them. Jackie pulled three ice-cold bottles of Coca-Cola from the fridge, and Mr. Rodriguez opened them all with a snap. Juanita counted out the coins despite Annie's pleas of "Let me pay!" They walked home, pouring Pop Rocks into their mouths. The girls admired the Ring Pops on their fingers. Jackie had a green Ring Pop, her favorite color. Juanita and Annie had red ones, and they teased Jackie, singing, "We are the ruby sisters. You are the emerald sister. The wicked witch." They raced back to Abuelo's house. Juanita came in first, Annie second, and Jackie third.

Their mom was listening to Abuelo as she folded his laundry when they walked into the house. Abuelo had a picture of their abuela who had died when their mom was fourteen. Underneath the picture was a cream-colored hand-crocheted doily.

"Your grandpa is telling me how Grandma used to help run their dairies. She handled all the money."

"Please, Abuelo, tell us about Abuela," the girls said, crowding around the faded picture.

"Tu abuela era muy inteligente con las matemáticas. Como tu mamá..." Mom translated, "Your grandmother was so intelligent in math. Just like your mom."

The girls nodded as they bit into crispy Pioneer Chicken legs, ate their candy, downed their Coca-Colas, and listened as their mom translated stories about their abuela, a few sentences at a time.

After sunset, the girls hugged their abuelo goodbye. He smelled of cigarettes and sweat, just like Daddy. They waved rather than spoke their goodbyes as they drove down the dusty road back home. Their mom's favorite song came on, and they all sang along to "Coal Miner's Daughter" by Loretta Lynn, pinching and giggling all the way home.

Looking back, I really wish that my mom had taught us Spanish so we could have heard Grandpa's stories directly. I know my father was against my mom teaching us Spanish. I know my mother's knuckles were slapped with a ruler every time she spoke Spanish in school. So it is understandable why she did not teach us.

These years at the continuation school where I still currently teach have been the best teaching years of my entire career. Still, there have been challenges, especially when I was out for a week due to Covid.

Emo's Missing!

Picture this: It was August 8th, 2021. The bell rang, and as I looked out at the sea of faces, they looked back at me. Even before I met them, I knew it was going to be a special year. I had collected shells on the beaches of Miami and visualized beautiful, open-hearted, teachable souls.

"Okay, so I'm Jacqueline Marie Mantz Rodriguez, but you can call me 'Dr. Mantz' or 'Ms. Mantz.' Let's go around the room and tell me the name you would like to be called," I said. As the students said their names, I nodded and repeated them back to ensure I had pronounced them correctly. I smiled, looking directly into their eyes. This year was different; we were all different after Covid. As an English and history teacher at a continuation high school, our classroom was set up more like a yoga studio than a traditional classroom. Mandalas and colorful tapestries adorned the walls. Students could choose to sit at a desk or on a mat. Cold water was provided, and we honored four agreements: Be impeccable with your word, don't take anything personally, don't make assumptions, and always do your best.

At the beginning of every class period on the first day, students would find a mint and a gratitude card on their desks. I was ready to abandon the authoritarian model of teaching. It was time to set myself and the students free. I was prepared to invite young people to embark on a journey with me. Were the students ready? By Friday of the first week of school, we were slightly more comfortable with each other. I shared stories from my life, and students reciprocated, telling me about theirs.

They wrote about who they were and how they had ended up in continuation school. When I read their stories, it opened my heart even more. I reaffirmed my vow to make our classroom a safe, calm place—a sanctuary of learning and peace.

I asked the students to pick a shell and write one of the mantras we had learned on it. Amelia chose the word "calm" and smiled as she held the shell in her hand. Breath by breath, day by day, we created our "stamily"—a community of learners supporting one another to succeed in school. Jessica, one of the students who had initially used colorful language, transformed into a prolific writer whose poem was eventually published in a literary magazine.

I made time to listen. If a student needed someone to listen to them, I would instruct the others to engage in a quiet writing activity. I'll never forget when Jose approached me with pain in his eyes, expressing his emotions about the loss of his grandfather. I listened.

You might be wondering, when did I teach? I taught all the time, but students' social-emotional health was prioritized, especially given the challenges many of us, including myself, had faced. I found liberation in making social-emotional learning a foundational part of my classroom, focusing on modern writers of color and developing students' writing skills.

I had preconceived notions of what a continuation school was, likely influenced by too many movies: *Stand and Deliver*, *Dangerous Minds*, and *Freedom Writers*. The continuation school model had changed within the last few years. We were moving away from independent studies to actively teaching and supporting students in their academic and personal needs. What I realized is that I was no savior. Students needed to save themselves. They needed someone who cared deeply to guide them in their learning. By October, we were closer than any of my previous classes. By winter break, we had become a strong "stamily."

Our class mascot, Emo—a troll doll my dad had given me before he passed away—was always present, sitting on my desk. Emo, with his red hair and blue eyes, would sometimes reprimand students for misbehaving, echoing my words about the importance of respectful behavior.

In January, new students joined us, and in April, our class size grew again, yet we continued to bond and grow together. I was honored as Teacher of the Year for the school and then as District Teacher of the Year. My life felt like a dream until I contracted Covid during spring break. I was out for the first week of school, and upon my return, I was still feeling exhausted and drained. It was on a Tuesday that I realized Emo, our class mascot, was missing.

I've been puppeteering my entire life, using voices with puppets and dolls. Most of my students tolerated Emo, and some even placed him on their desks as they worked. The last time I had seen him, he was wearing his soccer outfit. Despite our efforts to find him, Emo was nowhere to be found in the classroom.

Emo, who was around twenty years old but never aged, had a unique personality. He was a cross between Bart Simpson and Chuckie. My daddy had won Emo for me during a breakfast at Denny's. Daddy loved games, and the claw machine was no exception. He had inserted a dollar, and just like that, Emo was born. Daddy is gone now, and my inheritance includes Emo, a belt buckle with the name John on it, and a plastic Big Mouth

Billy Bass mounted on faux wood that was supposed to sing but had stopped working.

I never imagined Emo would be "trollnapped." My classroom was a place of trust. I told the kids, "Mi clase es su clase." The week I was absent, some kids had hid another student's phone in the classroom. The phone was eventually found, but I couldn't help but wonder if these incidents were connected.

My mind raced with thoughts. Trust, something I had cultivated with my students, had been violated. Where do we go from here? I wrote an email to the staff, pleading for Emo's return.

Hello,

This may sound amusing, but it's not. While I was away, my troll doll Emo, who serves as our class mascot and was a gift from my late father, went missing. Please speak to your classes and help bring him home.

Thank you,

Jackie

Fifteen minutes later, our principal's voice echoed over the intercom, urging whoever had taken Emo to return him. She called him "Elmo," but the kids understood. Thursday evening, I called my mom and shared the news of Emo's theft.

"What's wrong with them! Aren't there computers? Tell them what I did to you when you stole," she exclaimed. "I don't condone violence in my class, Mom," I replied.

Friday morning, my twin sister Juanita and I lamented Emo's disappearance. She created a flier to aid in the search. Exhausted, having not slept all night due to dreams of my father and my beloved dog Harper Lee, I put up the flyers during my prep period. Throughout the day, students asked, "Is Emo back yet?" During lunch, students came to speak with me, expressing their concern. Jessica sat down beside me, asking about Emo.

"No Emo yet," I said. During my fourth-period world history class, one of my students, Jim, told me to look inside his backpack as he handed it to me. There was Emo, staring back at me with his bright blue eyes. I put Emo behind my desk and took a deep breath.

"Thank you, Jim. I know you didn't take him. I appreciate you getting him back," I said. Jim did not take Emo, but one of his homies had. I looked around my room and sighed. A sick feeling filled my stomach and rose like a swarm into my throat making me cough and gag.

The students were silent and began filling out their vocabulary cards, all except for Sunny. She came up to me and began to cry. "I'm so mad. The kids were being horrible all week to the substitute and left a mess. I cleaned your whole classroom. There was trash on the floor, and the sub let the kids just grab the candy out of your bucket. Then, they took Emo. I love my stuffed animals, and they give me so much comfort. I am glad you got him back."

I gave Sunny a side hug and told her, "Thank you for caring so much. I'm sorry I got emotional. You are an empathetic person, and I'm so glad you are my student. I really appreciate you cleaning up the room. Go ahead and work in the side room. Do you want some tea?"

"Just water," said Sunny. As I walked around helping students with their vocabulary, Manuel raised his hand.

"Ms. Mantz, can I speak to you?"

I nodded, and he came up to my desk and sat down and whispered, "I think people are saying I took Emo. I didn't."

"I know you didn't take him Manuel but talk to me outside at the door," I said. I left the door propped open as we spoke.

"Ms. Mantz, I know your dad gave you Emo. I would never take him," Manuel said.

"I believe you, Manuel, and I know you didn't take him," I said. "It's okay. Emo is back, and we are moving on."

The weekend passed, and I meditated on the issue. I spoke to my sponsor and thought about how to move forward. On Monday, I spoke to every class. We discussed the cost of theft and trust. Students wrote about a time they had had their trust broken. Many of them had been stolen from or lied to by friends and family. As I read their stories, I resolved to start the year with lessons on trust. There is always a lesson. I learned that we can pour ourselves into teaching, but these incidents will happen. I am just one teacher doing the best I can with what I have. I have so much to give. I did beautiful work by opening my heart and being my authentic self. I refuse to give in to negativity and distrust. During the last week of school, it was Spirit Week and Emo had on his red Angels jersey and hat. I locked him in the cupboard and turned off the lights. Then I heard Emo's voice from the cupboard.

"Mom, where's Stevo? I haven't seen my little puppet friend since I got back to class. Remember the one Grandma got you for Christmas. He was taken also," Emo said. As I walked away, I thought, we need to pick our battles.

Sunny became the cover designer and editor of the school literary journal I curate. She graduated in 2022, and we continue to stay in touch. Sunny is in a long-term relationship. She plans to attend community college and wants to be a tattoo artist. Sunny and I collaborated, and she designed the images on the cover of this book. I paid her, of course, as artists deserve to be paid for their work.

Kindness on Credit

Some students are harder to get along with than others. Miguel was one of those students I had to remind myself, on a daily basis, to treat with firm kindness, as he and I always seemed at odds. He would push boundaries by constantly asking to go to the bathroom, attempting to leave thirty seconds before the bell rang, and hiding certain students' possessions as if we were playing a game of hide-and-seek rather than attending school.

His energy would often propel him out of his seat. Wherever he went, voices raised in protest. I did my best not to react and rarely sent him to the office, knowing this would damage any chance of a positive relationship. He irritated me. My irritation disturbed me more than his actions because I had cultivated positive relationships with most of my students. Additionally, I suspected he was the one who had kidnapped Emo, my troll doll. I called his aunt about his behavior, and that worked, at least for about a week.

Back then, I taught history and enjoyed it. In the first history unit, we studied ancient civilizations, and I assigned an essay to the class. Miguel finished his essay first but refused to type it out; instead, he rewrote it by hand. I allowed this, as a few students preferred writing by hand, even if it meant rewriting a piece twice after my review. I displayed his essay on the bulletin board with a sticker, to which he responded, "Stickers are for kids." He then spent three days texting underneath his desk, pretending to work on assignments from Civics.

"Do you want me to look over your Civics essay for you?"

"Nope, I'm good." I knew he was failing Mr. Rodriguez's Civics class, as I pulled all his grades and met with him regarding them. Alas, I had twenty other students' essays to review with them.

I rewarded students with the movie *Babe*, one of my favorites and the topic of the opinion piece I planned to use to assess their growth as writers.

On Wednesday, we finished the movie. The students had difficulty paying attention to the film, although they appreciated the rousing ending. On Thursday, we learned how to write an opinion piece. But I could tell there were some other activities happening underneath my radar. A teacher always has a sixth sense. During this instruction, I accidentally allowed my airdrop app to be open. The science teacher and I were texting back and forth about specific students going to the bathroom. I accidentally allowed a picture to be air-dropped. The kids were shamefaced when I screamed as the picture popped up. They worked quietly as I documented the incident in an email.

On Friday, when students walked into history class, I stated, "You have the class period to write your opinion piece. You can write about the movie or another topic you have a strong opinion about. This is a writing assessment to see how well you can write independently." I passed out Thinking Maps to support their brainstorming process.

Ten minutes into the class period, Amelia ran out of the class without permission. Lisa asked, "Can I go after her?" I opened the door and saw Amelia sitting on a bench speaking to her boyfriend, Oscar.

"We're good, Lisa. She is talking to someone," I said. I called security, and Amelia came back fifteen minutes later and approached me.

"Can I speak to you in the back room privately?" We walked into the back room, and I closed the door. My classroom is a teacher's dream, with a small kitchen area with huge glass windows, allowing me to see outside the room while speaking to students privately.

"Dr. Mantz, I left because I was so damn angry," said Amelia. Her speech picked up pace. "Oscar gave me his debit card, so I could go get snacks at 7-Eleven after school. He has to work. I had it on the desk, and Miguel grabbed it. When I tried to grab it back, it broke. You know I have anger problems, and I'm working on them, but he made me so mad. I just want to apologize for walking out." Her voice cracked, and she looked up at me with the eyes of a dove.

"Amelia, you did the right thing. I'm proud of you," I said. She began to cry. Her shoulders heaved as I patted her back. Lisa sat in the back of the room with Amelia for the rest of the class, as I wanted to keep Miguel and Amelia separate. The counselor called Miguel up to speak to him about the incident. Right before the class ended, Miguel returned.

As the students walked out, Miguel passed by me at the door. Oscar, Amelia's boyfriend and the owner of the broken credit card, saw Miguel and ordered, "Come here!" Miguel looked at me. I looked at him. Time moved in slow motion. Oscar's fist came up to Miguel's face. Miguel's head popped back and forth as Oscar's fists connected in rapid succession. Oscar had recently shown me videos of his boxing workouts. He outweighed Miguel by twenty pounds.

"Go get security," I called out as I jumped between them, and Oscar stopped in mid-punch. Two other boys grabbed Oscar and Miguel. Steve, the security guard, ran up and grabbed Miguel and took him to the office to get a statement.

“Keep Oscar here. I will inform the principal that he is in your room,” Steve said. Oscar walked into the room; I propped open the door with a trash can, and we sat and waited for his mom. Oscar was a polite, quiet man who always said, “Yes ma’am.” The week before, he had worn dark Tone Loc sunglasses in class, and I saw a black eye when he lowered his glasses to acknowledge me. I knew there was some anger brewing in him from other issues.

“I’m sorry, Dr. Mantz. I lost my temper. My mom’s going to be pissed off,” he said. He wrote his statement and took full responsibility. As he walked out of the room with his mom, I said, “Take this time to think about how we can work on this, Oscar. You can learn from this. I know it. Make sure you do the work in Google Classroom, if you aren’t here for the next few days.” He nodded, and I watched him walk out with his mom toward the office. He ended up being suspended for three days. After Oscar left, I went up to the office. The administration asked me to walk Miguel out to his aunt’s car.

“Are you okay?” I asked.

“I have a bump on my head,” Miguel whimpered. Miguel returned the next day. I pulled him aside and asked, “How are you?” He nodded and gave me a thumbs up. Since that day, Miguel no longer sought to get a reaction out of me. We had a truce of sorts brought about by the fight.

Miguel graduated high school in 2023. His sister attended our school too, so she updated me all the time. “Miguel is going to have a baby,” she said to me the other day. Amelia, Oscar’s girlfriend, moved to Arizona before the end of the year. When Oscar graduated, he followed her over there. I picture them eating chorizo and eggs in their small apartment away from the cycle of trauma that had infested their lives. As educators, we encounter students, each with their own unique story. While some students readily share their experiences, others choose not to, perhaps due to personal reasons. It's common for people to make assumptions about each other. It's a daily goal for me to remind myself that I don't know what challenges any student may have faced before entering our classroom. We all have our stories.

I Have a Bat

I have a bat
from softball practice
in the closet by my desk
just in case
we go on lockdown

I have a bat
I don't want to use it
but I will
damn
I haven't had the talk with kids
this year, yet

I have a bat
I put in my closet after
active shooter training
not called H.E.R.O. training, anymore
ridiculous acronyms
to numb the horror
remember, I can't even remember
so many names

I have a bat
a red fire extinguisher
heavy dumbbells

use anything, to live
I WILL do anything to let my kids live

Must talk to them today
in a circle about what to do
when we must do something

WE must choose
fight for our right for life
I'll Slim Shady that piece of shit

Pray, I'll pray now so then I'll
channel a miracle
stand at a door
with that metal bat in hand
ready, I'm ready to die
to protect
AND
I'll go down swinging

I strive to make connections with all students, but some need more support. Juliet was one of these students. We connected through writing, food, and our dreams.

A Dreamer

Juliet gazed at the wall, her pale head resting on her hands, her long eyelashes still wet with glue, lost in dreams. In class, she was always hungry, often asking for a second mint, and halfway through, inquiring, "Dr. Mantz, do you have any granola bars?" After eating, she would hurriedly dash to the bathroom. Birdlike with long brown hair, she was a delicate creature.

At lunch, I opened my classroom doors for all students to have somewhere cool to eat. Juliet and I laughed as we examined our lunches; we both adored sriracha on everything. On other days, Juliet would fast and doze off during class. One day, she appeared particularly fatigued, prompting me to ask, "How are you?"

"My aunt says I look amazing since I lost weight, but I'm not feeling well," she replied. I listened as she shared her struggles with food, nodding in understanding. Her situation resonated with me; she could have been me. I struggled with disordered eating my entire life. It is something I work on daily: allowing myself to eat without guilt or purging. According to recent studies, approximately ten percent of women in the United States struggle with some form of eating disorder; anorexia nervosa, bulimia nervosa, and binge-eating disorder, being among the most common diagnoses. Moreover, research indicates that eating disorders often manifest during adolescence and young adulthood.

During lunch, Juliet confided in me about her family, her new boyfriend, and her life. On tough days, she would work in the back room to ensure she could graduate on time with the class of 2022. Juliet wrote poetry in the elective meditation/writing class I taught. Every Wednesday, students would gather for an hour and a half, starting with a meditation session followed by writing prompts. We would compose poems, journals, and letters to ourselves. Juliet was a pensive, deliberate writer. When she submitted her work, she would often say, "It's not good. I'm gonna throw it away." I would encourage her to type it out, review it for minor edits, and display it on the wall with a comment from me, such as, "Lovely word choice and imagery." Her writings, along with those of the other students, inspired me to start a literary journal, aiming to honor and publish students' words.

Juliet would sometimes disappear for days, only to return to catch up on missed assignments. Before handing her a stack of work, I would often crack a silly joke.

"What did the mama tomato do and say to the baby tomato as they were walking across the street, and the baby tomato was lagging behind?" I asked.

"No, Mrs. Mantz, not again. Okay, what?" she groaned.

"She stomped on her head and said, 'Ketchup, ketchup.'"

"You are so silly," Juliet said.

"I know, please come in at lunch and get your work caught up," I urged.

Then, Juliet found a job and switched to independent study. As the year drew to a close, I discussed her progress with the independent study teacher.

"She only has a P.E. log to complete, along with an essay, and she hasn't turned in anything, so she may not graduate," the teacher informed me. With only two weeks until graduation, I called Juliet's home, and she answered.

"Juliet, you need to turn in your work to your independent study teacher," I said urgently. "Let me speak to your mom."

"Okay, I've just been working a lot. I'll come Friday," Juliet promised and handed the phone to her mom. After speaking with Juliet's mom using Google Translator, I reiterated the importance of her meeting the deadline. On Friday at 3 p.m., she showed up just as the independent study teacher was leaving. Juliet turned in her work, and on graduation night, she walked across the stage. I sighed and prayed a silent affirmation for her dreams, believing they were now closer to reality.

Juliet and I kept in touch. She informed me that her job as a waitress in a family-owned restaurant kept her tips but paid her eighteen dollars an hour.

"You need to find a new job," I advised her. My friends in the area provided several job leads. However, one friend's suggestion was met with concern from Juliet.

"Ms. Mantz, I don't have papers. I can't work there," she confessed. I was at a loss for words, unsure of how to navigate this issue or offer assistance. After a few days of silence, she contacted me again, saying, "I got let go from my job. I'm applying to College of the Desert, but I need to work to help my family with bills." Juliet's situation mirrors that of many young people after high school graduation. Even Deferred Action for Childhood Arrivals (DACA) does not offer a path to citizenship and is constantly under threat.

As a young girl, I dreamed of creating a better life for myself—one with a career I loved, a home of my own, and a family. Through hard work, attending college and university, finding teaching, and achieving sobriety, my dreams came true. When I think of Juliet's aspirations for a better life, I'm left staring at a blank wall. As a teacher, I am ill-equipped to navigate the complexities of DACA. But I did try to find someone to help Juliet.

Did you know that as of 2023 there are over 500,000 DACA recipients in the United States, each with their own story and aspirations? One of my co-workers is a "Dreamer." Yes, there are many staff and teachers who are Dreamers. She advised Juliet to contact a local group of advocates for DACA recipients in the Coachella Valley. I sent Juliet the number and hoped. But hope is not enough for these young people anymore. We need action. I urge anyone who disagrees with DACA to get to know one person under DACA. Talk to people, listen to their stories, and your heart will open. I believe we fear what we do not understand. We must start talking and listening to one another if we have any hope of saving humanity and the planet.

During my lunch recently, I was summoned to the front office. There stood Juliet, holding a Starbucks coffee.

"Hi, Dr. Mantz, I just wanted to thank you for everything. I got you a coffee and a cake pop," she said. We sat in the front office and caught up for a few minutes.

"Thanks, Juliet, you've made my day. It's lovely to be remembered and appreciated. I love a flat white latte," I responded.

"Of course, Ms. Mantz. I always remember the advice and kindness you showed me. A big part of why I was able to leave my relationship is because I remembered. I appreciate you so much," Juliet expressed. Currently, she is working and attending community college. I encouraged her to take writing classes since she wasn't fond of the business courses offered. After all, she is a dreamer.

Pockets of Creation

We sat in a circle and sipped our chamomile tea, five females bound together by a love of the written word. We smiled at one another as we ingested warmth and prepared ourselves for the day's writing workshop class. All these young female writers were students at a continuation school.

Our journey to this moment was a result of suffering. I was no exception. My own struggles during the time of Covid brought me back home to teaching. During these dark times of loss and suffering, I decided to step down from administration and return to the classroom. A twenty-year special education English teacher, I finally received the opportunity to use my general education English teaching credential. It took what it took. To find one’s purpose is everything and worth it all. My students in this class were all once at the comprehensive high school, but during Covid, many of them failed classes. So here we were, all together in this lavender-scented room. There are no lit candles allowed in a school classroom due to the fire alarms. Yet, teachers are inventive, so I had a coffee cup heater plugged into the wall, and I put my scented candle on it. The candles lasted forever and reminded me of how beautiful teaching bends time.

We came from different perspectives and realities, but the one thing we all had in common was we had chosen this class. We chose to write. The premise of this weekly ninety-minute class was simple, yet deeper than any ocean’s depths. We met every week for nine weeks. We drank hot tea, meditated, studied a topic, and then responded to a writing prompt. The goal was to write weekly, and by the end of the course, edit one piece for submission to a literary journal.

Classes such as this felt magical, as if I had dreamed into being a group of sensitive souls able to wield a pen like a sword, cutting the many layers of their experiences into bite-sized sounds and images. These fellow women of the pen made me proud to sit in this room and help guide them through the experience of writing.

During the silent writing portion of our class, we usually listened to the singer Lana Del Rey. The students could respond to the prompts in the form of a letter, a song, a poem, or a story that was fiction or nonfiction. Some of us would write while sitting on our mats, and others at desks. We would warm our tea without a word. The goal was to free the students of the constraints of an educational institution. To make them feel like they were coming home to a sacred space within themselves.

One particular day, we studied self-compassion and wrote letters to ourselves about our greatest suffering. We wrote words of comfort to ourselves as if we were compassionate friends. We listened with attentive ears and eyes as each writer shared their work. We snapped our fingers in gratitude after each person read. Those letters, those lovely, heart-breaking letters that I cannot read to you, made me clear my throat and heave a deep sigh.

To be vulnerable and authentic with one's students is to feel as if one is climbing up the tallest tree in the wind. Teachers underestimate the power of authenticity and vulnerability. After twenty-two years in education, I am finally able to lower the mask and share my own writing. It has made all the difference, as students now have a model. They can decide to be vulnerable and their most authentic selves in their writings.

"Why don't we see ourselves as others see us?" one writer asked. No oracle am I. I just listened then asked questions. We all handwrote our letters. If this were any other day, I would have asked the writers to type their pieces. That day I did not. These letters were sacred and belonged solely to each writer.

"Find a safe place to keep your letter," I said. I put mine in my handbag in the zippered compartment. The writers carefully folded up their letters and put them into pockets in their backpacks or purses. None of these letters may ever be seen or heard again. These letters may be too bright with pain for others to see or they may someday be uncaged to fly out again into the word sky of the writer's world.

Circles of Love

The rain falls as my fear rises. Fear over the tropical storm warning, fear over catastrophe. I'm a romantic and a catastrophic thinker. When I was a child, I would read, and read, and read. I wasn't picky as library books were great but so were the boxes of books people gave my daddy. He worked for Mayflower, a moving company. He loved free stuff as did I. I'm the teacher who goes to conferences ready to collect swag. I developed my romanticism by reading boxes of Harlequin romance novels. As kids, my twin and I would trade books back and forth, marveling at especially well-done ones within the genre.

"Can you believe he ravished her in the pool? I'm going to write for Harlequin when I grow up," Juanita said.

"No, I'm going to write for Harlequin," I retorted.

My catastrophic thinking is a result of many factors. I am sure the dysfunction of my parents fighting a lot contributed to it. Yes, drinking alcohol until I got sober at the age of thirty-seven also contributed. And even other traumas I lived through played a role. I'm fascinated by dystopian books and movies. Maybe I'm addicted, addicted to fear's rising.

What does this have to do with teaching? We all have stories, experiences, and even trauma that inform our teaching practices. In the past, I kept my truths in a side pocket of a deep, dark purse. Today, my truth lies inside a yoga pants pocket, ready to emerge and fly like a bird to land on the tree of the present moment.

Today is Sunday, and I have no idea if I will make it to school tomorrow. There's flooding, a jury duty notice, and uncertainty. Everything is okay, right now. This allows me peace and time to plan for next week. Every school year, the district has a focus. This year, it is equity and restorative teaching practices. My heart and mind blossomed like a hibiscus flower when I went to the training on restorative teaching practices. It reminded me of the power of "teaching circles."

During the first three days of school, we sat in discussion circles. In this practice, there was a "talking piece" so each student would have the opportunity to speak and to be listened to by their peers and educators. Active listening is important. I listened to students all week in these ten-minute circles we do at the beginning of each class period. We created norms, got to know one another, and checked in with each other regarding our emotions. This proactive approach is essential to building trust and relationships so that when incidents happen, students and teachers have a tool to turn to in times of conflict.

Monday morning of the second week I organized the Chromebook cart. I noticed there was a computer missing. The classroom phone rang. I answered with my catchphrase, "This is Jackie Mantz, how may I help you?"

"Jackie, I'm missing a Chromebook," said Ms. Tan, the science teacher. "Can you let me know if anyone turns one in, please?"

"I'm missing a Chromebook too, uh oh," I said. I'm human. When these events happen, my first thought is to lecture rather than talk with the students. We all do this in classes. I do this in my class, and it has its place. But, since we had been already doing the circles, I decided to address the missing Chromebook within the circle. I had a chapter to read and discuss with the kids, but this was more important. We could continue *The Four Agreements* by Don Miguel Ruiz after the circle discussion. We started with a review of our norms.

All of us sit in a circle.

The person holding the talking piece is the only one talking.

We listen actively and technology is put away.

You can pass if the question is too personal.

If you need more "think time," we can circle back to you.

As I held the talking piece, this time Mr. Snuffleupagus, I said, "Say one feeling word related to having something stolen from you. I'll start, loss." I passed the stuffed animal.

"Traumatic, can you come back, brutal, loss of trust, anger, sadness, disbelief, trifling, umm disloyal..." The words poured out of students. The animal returned to me after all the students shared their words. Then I told my story of Emo being stolen.

"See my troll Emo, he was given to me by my daddy right before he died of pancreatic cancer. A couple of years ago, I caught Covid and was out for a week. When I got back, Emo was missing. I tore up the classroom, but he was gone. We had a circle just like this one today. Emo came back after a week. I was so grateful to the student who had brought him back. Emo is a doll, I know he's not alive, but he is the only inheritance besides my huge heart that I have from my daddy." The students nodded. I passed Mr. Snuffleupagus to the left.

"Pass," the first kid said.

"I got my bike stolen last year. I worked on that bike for years, so it was brutal when it got stolen." He passed the stuffed toy.

"Pass." "Pass." "My best friend stole from me one day after we went to the mall. She was stealing stuff from the stores, but I didn't think she'd do it to me. It was so shady for her to go through my purse and take my wallet when I wasn't looking when she was at my house. My mom saw her. We aren't friends anymore as I told her that friends don't do that stuff. She's out." We finished our circle with information and a request from me.

"So, I will be counting the Chromebooks at the end of each period. One is missing, and I hope it is returned as I choose to believe someone borrowed it. Before we leave our circle and get to reading *The Four Agreements*, let's conclude the circle with one word on how you feel."

"Love them, communicate, sad, uncomfortable, okay, cool, emotional..." A student came up to me later in the day and handed me a Chromebook.

"This was in your back room." I walked to the cart and checked the missing number. It was not one of mine. I called Ms. Tan.

"Are you missing Chromebook number seven?"

"Yes!" At the end of the day, we were all in corpse pose meditating when security walked into the class. "I found this Chromebook in the bathroom. Someone said it is yours," he said. I got up and took it to the cart. It was the missing Chromebook number twelve. We were engaged in our yoga class. Students continued to breathe in and out, lying in savasana as I breathed in and out gratitude. In this present moment, I'm grateful for shelter, safety, reflection, and communication, which can turn fear into love.

Resting Corpses

Resting corpses lie on mats around the classroom
restoring balance to our day
lights low, soft music floats around the room
we are face-up on the ground, arms and legs
comfortably spread, eyes closed.

Savasana?
Yes, savasana.

Mind, body, breath, spirit rests
we scan our bodies
moving from our toes, up through our legs.

Letting breath and body unite, restore balance
we are still silent seesaws
giggles bubble up and move from corpse
to corpse as white light moves up
into shoulders and necks

Relax your jaw, relax your cheeks, relax your eyebrows
and the space between the eyebrows, the third eye
we rest in savasana.

Moz Moments

One weekend in Vegas, I saw Morrissey, "Moz," in concert. Morrissey is the former lead vocalist of The Smiths but has had a long solo career. I have seen Morrissey in concert at least five times. Even at a concert in Vegas, I am always on the lookout for inspiration.

For a lifelong teacher like me, teachable moments are like hidden treasures, emerging unexpectedly from the depths of everyday life. They beckon students with vibrant hues of green and orange, far more enticing than any novel or expository passage. That's why I had previously tucked a vegan informational flier into my handbag; I knew I had struck educational gold upon reading the quote from Morrissey emblazoned on the front: "Your decision is whether you support the butcher or the butchered. It cannot be both."

Monday arrived, and I laid out the article along with letter-writing templates and a mint on each desk, a small gesture to ease the flow of thoughts. Writing letters has been my forte; I penned my book in collaboration with a soul confined behind bars, exchanging emails as our mode of connection. I've corresponded with many of my favorite authors and poured my thoughts onto my blog—a letter of sorts to the world.

"Why do I hear cows, Dr. Mantz?" a student quipped.

"Well, 'Meat is Murder' is the title of this song," I replied. "Let's delve into the article from PETA urging us to consider veganism. Afterward, you'll craft a letter to Morrissey, expressing your thoughts."

"Do we have to agree?" someone asked.

"No," I affirmed. "Your opinions matter. Whether you agree or disagree, articulate what you truly believe." We delved into the article together, punctuated by the backdrop of Smiths songs, each tackling pertinent social issues. "The Headmaster Ritual" critiqued corporal punishment, while "That Joke Isn't Funny Anymore" delved into themes of loneliness and suicide.

In addition to the PETA article, I introduced another piece offering counter arguments against veganism, outlining perspectives that challenged the lifestyle choice. It was imperative for students to consider a spectrum of viewpoints to foster critical thinking and informed decision-making.

The following day, I had students read aloud their letters to a peer. They gave one positive comment about the piece and asked a question on the content of the letter. After they met with their peers, I met with students one-on-one to discuss their piece's strengths and to suggest areas of improvement. This process not only honed their writing skills but also encouraged empathy and understanding as they listened to their peers' viewpoints along with my input.

The letters poured forth with honesty. Some were courteous, others unabashedly forthright, and a few even injected with humor. Yet, each bore the imprint of the student's unique perspective and experiences regarding veganism. I stapled all the letters around Morrissey's concert poster.

I too penned a letter, envisioning a moment where I might hand-deliver these missives to Morrissey himself. Perhaps one evening, I'll be that woman, pleading for him to accept the envelope at the foot of the stage.

When the 2023–2024 school year ended, we had one final circle. In that circle we had on the last day, I shared my goal of obtaining additional certifications in yoga by going on a yoga retreat for two weeks in Joshua Tree. Then I shared my favorite moment of the year. Typically, I would share about graduation. But this year, it was not about graduation. It was one of those moments that I hope to carry into the ever after. It was a moment filled with star stuff.

Star Stuff

> "The cosmos is within us. We are made of star stuff. We are a way for the universe to know itself." —Carl Sagan

Within us lie vast multitudes, layers upon layers of quilted ideas stitched together. Our lives are pages upon pages of the mundane, the irritating, the gasp-worthy beautiful. I am a teacher; some days come and go, but others remain in golden memory.

Yesterday, I stapled handmade books together, swearing within as my printer lost its bearings and its plastic parts burst out. My anxiety kicked up a notch, but then the bell rang. The spell of gloom and doom lifted, dispelled by purpose—the purpose of infusing a love of reading into small, starry-eyed preschool children.

For weeks, our high school creative writing class worked on writing and illustrating children's stories. Each had a positive message for young children and included hand-drawn illustrations. Students could work with partners or individually. The stories were unique and illustrated with care.

Mia and Martino, high school sweethearts, worked together on a story entitled "Big Bob" about an elementary-age chubby lowrider vehicle bullied by young cars and trucks for being fat. Big Bob runs away to a park only to be mentored by older Chicano trucks that take him back to school. My favorite part was the story's ending: "'Woo Woo, wow, órale,' cried the little cars and trucks. From that day, Big Bob was never made fun of again!" Mia and Martino drew detailed Monte Carlo cars and Chevy trucks. I knew young children would love the pictures and authentic cultural language.

Erica, a senior student, wrote a story about a sunflower with different-colored petals and long eyelashes. The sunflower's mother taught her the value of self-love. Erica painted her pictures using watercolors, and the sunset-hued sunflowers shone on the page. After we were close to finishing our stories, Erica asked, "Can we read them to the preschool students? I volunteer there, and the school is next door to us."

After I informed Erica that her idea was approved, she said, "Ms. Mantz, I think I want to be a preschool teacher after I graduate." She swung her auburn hair to the side and laughed, "I don't think I could tolerate high school, but working with the little ones is so much fun." She then reapplied her glittering rose lipstick and checked her image on her cell phone.

My heart was racing, and I closed my eyes for a moment. Time is our most precious resource, and this project ran out of it. It was frustrating as some students needed to print their stories the day of the reading, and my printer was now like a broken WALL-E.

"Ms. Mantz, it'll be okay," said Roberto. "Just practice that breathing you tell us to do when we get stressed out." I took three breaths in through the nose and out through the mouth. I grabbed my lavender essential oils and rubbed some on my wrists.

Mr. Lenny, the English as a Second Language paraeducator, said, "I can print the remaining ones using the library's printer." He had been there throughout the last month helping students refine their stories. He was from El Salvador and was working on his master's degree. He walked over to Luis and Lesenia, another high school power couple, and said, "Necesitas tu historia, ¿verdad? Vamos a la biblioteca." Then, like Emiliano Zapata, he led the charge to the library. They came back soon with printed copies of the last stories. We finished putting together the last book at 1:30 p.m. The bell rang at 1:35, and the students stayed as they had been excused from their sixth-period class for the event. I typically taught yoga during this period. There was no funding for a one-period substitute so the yoga students would go with us to the library. Two of those students used inappropriate language, so I sent them to another room to do their work.

"Whatever. I have lil' brothers and sisters. I know how to act right," Marie said as she flounced away. I wanted to say that if you acted right in class, I wouldn't need to do this, but I just waved to her. Sometimes, silence is more powerful than a retort.

At 1:45 p.m., the students in our creative writing class took their books to the library. I wished our orderly but sterile library had been decorated to make it more appealing. But our library technician was only there two days a week. Roberto looked at me, cleared his throat, and said in a squeaky voice, "Is it normal to feel nervous?" I laughed and replied, "I am still nervous every time I read my writings." The students all smiled as they saw the four-year-old boys and girls sitting in a circle with their teacher, such tiny, trusting beings.

"Oh, they are so cute," said Teresa. "Can we read to that little boy over there, Dr. Mantz?"

"Yeah, I wanna read to him too. He reminds me of my little brother," said William. I nodded, and Teresa and William sat on the floor, and the little boy sat on a blue bean bag chair. The little boy wiggled and giggled as Teresa and William went page by page into their stories, pointing to the illustrations and reading the words aloud slowly. The boy swung his Nike-clad feet to and fro. He said, "E.T." when Teresa showed him the cover of her book with an emerald alien in a shiny spaceship on it. Teresa nodded, and the little one clapped as he listened to her tell the story of Rory, an alien who had come to Earth with a magic ring that helped him make friends.

The preschool teacher asked if we had any Spanish speakers to translate the stories to a student who did not understand English. A little girl with a puffy pink and blue coat stood close to her teacher, holding her hand. Her big brown eyes underneath her glasses were wide. Mona raised her hand and said, "I can read her mine in Spanish." She walked over, gently took her hand, and said, "Hola, mi nombre es Mona." The little girl smiled and sat down with Mona in two blue plastic chairs. I watched as she went from wide-mouthed to smiling as Mona read to her about a magic paintbrush a little girl uses to bring a brown-and-white puppy to life.

"Me gustan los perros," the little girl said to Mona. Mona nodded and walked her back to her teacher as other Spanish speakers were waiting to read their stories to her.

The rest of the teens settled into the task, lowered their voices, and turned the pages of the books for the kids. One little boy in a red sweater with dark curly hair could not stand still, so his teacher walked him over to Angie, who smiled, patted the chair next to her, and read her story about how everyone's hair is different. The little boy kept trying to leave, but the teacher would calmly bring him back to Angie, who had a future therapist's energy and smile.

The children moved around, trading places to hear different stories. Some of the preschoolers shuffled their feet as they walked over to a new reader. The air was filled with words read aloud amid the soft rustling of pages and the occasional burst of gasps and laughter. I even got to read two stories to a little girl who had braided hair with rainbow barrettes. She smiled when I read about a mouse who wanted some "cheese, please, bigger than him." Then, her eyes grew wide as I read to her about a hungry shark eating a lot of fish.

At the end of our time, the students presented the preschool teacher with the books, and she said to our class, "Thanks for reading your stories." She gathered the small children, and they all cried, "Thanks for the books!" My students high-fived the kids, and we went back to class. I was at a loss for words to tell them how much I appreciated them and the difference their stories may make in a child's life. I wish I had said, "The stories you wrote were lovely. Please keep writing your stories, they matter. YOU MATTER!"

We are made of star stuff. Bones are born dense with calcium. Our muscles are sculpted of carbon. The lungs allow inhaled oxygen into the blood and remove carbon dioxide from the blood. Nothing is truly wasted; inhaling and exhaling bring life: blood iron and hydrogen flow. Heavy with youthful hope, these teens had shared stories born from the oxygen of their imagination. I do not understand what stars or what I am made of yet. Still, I know life is an incandescent universe of star stuff.

Graduation Day

The staging area was filled with seniors adjusting their black gowns and golden tassels, repeatedly fanning themselves. Our graduation at the continuation school was held at the local comprehensive high school. The students were getting ready in a room reserved for actors before they performed on stage. Tonight was the graduating class of 2022's time to be recognized for their hard work. Graduation night marked their transition from students to graduates, a rite of passage both sublime and serious. I walked around the room, capturing selfies of graduates for my graduation photo wall next year. I took pictures of students with highly decorated graduation caps. One cap had roses sewn onto the border with a Virgin de Guadalupe image stitched on top. Another cap had "I Did It" in rhinestones. Student after student posed in their regalia. I gave each one a hug and passed out lucky red bracelets I had bought in Chinatown.

They did it. Somehow, they had found a way, day by day, through unprecedented times, to pass their classes and show up to celebrate their hard work.

As each graduate walked across the stage to receive their "diploma," staff screamed themselves hoarse. Graduates' dedications spoke of support and love from their family, friends, teachers, counselors, and school staff. Maria walked across the stage and stopped when her words were read aloud, "Thank you, Mom, for always standing by me even when I wanted to give up. This is for you." She made a heart with her hands and looked out across the audience to her mother. Another student I was close to, who almost did not graduate, Juliet, walked across the stage with a huge, glowing smile. The announcer read, "I want to thank every teacher who helped me this year. I will never forget you." Our eyes met and I smiled back at her.

That year was magical, a glittering and golden green light that set tonight aglow. The beauty of teaching is that every year is a new dawn, and I am honored to be a part of students' journeys. Tragedy and monstrous violence may blot out the sun, but if I focus my eyes on these graduates, life is beautiful.

Teaching Teachers

Now, as a teacher back in the classroom, I support new teachers in a variety of ways. I am a practicum supervisor and a professor for a special education credential program. I teach various special education courses, meet with the teachers every Wednesday on Zoom for two hours, and observe their teaching practices via video. It's a lot of work, but I love it. Yet, sometimes teachers in the intern program struggle. I try to be the person teachers can turn to in such times.

Power of an Hour

David was the sole special education teacher left on Zoom, as the rest of the students in the two hour-long intern practicum class departed to work on submitting their missing assignments, with my blessings. As a teacher, I understand the significance of time. In addition to working full-time as special education teachers, where they are expected to juggle two roles simultaneously, interns in this program attend class three nights a week. Special education teachers teach all day and then manage a caseload of students, as well as write, schedule, and hold IEP meetings. There are never enough hours in the day to accomplish all the work that needs to be done.

David, with his button-down, blue collared shirt, graying hair, and tired eyes, was an exceptional teacher. Having coached teachers for many years, I recognized him as being in the top ten percent. He excelled at building relationships and teaching the social studies curriculum. When I reviewed his lesson plans, I marveled at his ability to organize, scaffold, and teach social studies to students with disabilities. Watching the videos he uploaded into Canvas, I was impressed by his calm professionalism with the kids. He usually had a hint of a smile and ran an organized classroom.

Today, David was not smiling as he drove home, which is why he had stayed online with me. He could have left and pretended he was going to work on assignments, but he was honest and dedicated, so he stayed as all the other students logged off. This was his character.

"We can talk, and I can see how you are holding up," I said.

"Sure, I am doing okay. Well, maybe I'm not." He ran his hand over his face and sighed. "I've been really wondering about staying in teaching. This is my second year, and it's harder than last year, as I feel as if I'm just babysitting. There are so many levels, and I know my admin says I'm meeting their expectations, but I don't feel like I am meeting mine." Words poured out of him. I nodded and listened without interrupting. He continued.

"Like, I taught general ed in Texas and I loved it when a majority of the kids got the lesson. In my class now, they just don't get it. Just today, a girl in my class was hearing voices, so I stopped teaching and listened to her for twenty minutes. Yet, the admin wants to know what my objective is and checks to see if the standards are on the board. They expect me to teach, but there are just so many needs these kids have, not related to social studies," David said as I watched him with his seatbelt on even though he had not started driving home yet.

"Have you talked to your admin about your feelings?" I asked.

"My principal tells me to speak to my vice-principal as she knows. They do support me, but I just don't agree with the system. It just seems like they throw kids into classes without thinking, and then they expect me to do IEP after IEP meeting, which impacts my teaching. I've never felt more vulnerable."

"Tell me more, what do you mean by vulnerable?" I said.

"Maybe that's not the right word. I feel like I can never finish everything. No matter how much work I take home, I'm running behind. I don't know what I'm going to do, as I love getting up there with the kids." David's eyes opened and brightened.

"The other day I was jogging in place and one of the kids thought I was dancing. He started dancing with me, and we were both laughing. I love being silly with kids."

"There are some people, David, who are meant to be teachers, and you are one of them," I said with a soft voice and smile.

"That's what the wife and kids said to me. They encouraged me to teach as I did such a good job tutoring the kids with schoolwork. You know, the special education system reminds me of the foster care system. My wife and I adopted our two boys, but we wanted to adopt more children. The foster care system is broken, so we decided not to adopt as what we had to do just didn't make sense. I feel like this as a special ed teacher. It just doesn't make sense."

"David, I remember what a therapist once told me. I was going on and on about how I could not manage a specific issue in my job. She asked me to consider that maybe the job itself was unmanageable. I want you to know you are doing an incredible job in an unmanageable situation. This is the truth. It is not you, and you are an incredible person and teacher. I am sorry you are going through this right now."

"I feel better just talking about it like we were meant to chat tonight about this, as I don't know what I'm going to do. I just know I need to think about my future. But it's not like any of my other jobs were as rewarding. I love my work hours and the kids. So, I need to start driving home but thank you, Dr. Jackie, for listening."

"It was amazing talking to you, David. I just realized that I don't talk to all of you one-on-one enough. Have a good night." Right after I got off the Zoom, I sent an email to the students in the intern practicum course:

"Greetings, Teachers! I hope the gift of time helped. I wanted to reach out to offer one-on-one phone or Zoom meetings this week. I can listen, or we can chat about a specific issue. This is not mandatory, just an offer to support you. Have an amazing week. Jackie."

As a teacher of teachers, I forget how stressful this time of year is for new educators. If they can just get to Thanksgiving without quitting, the year begins to fly by, at least for some. Special educators have one of the highest rates of burnout. I know, it took me twenty years, but I finally burned out. I understand the Herculean task facing them. As a practicum supervisor and coach of new special education teachers, it is my duty to pay it forward by being the best mentor and coach possible. Sometimes people just want to be listened to as there are no simple solutions to the issue of special education in the United States.

David took a leave of absence from the intern program shortly after our conversation. I was angry, not at David, but at the system. We must support our teachers better and address the challenges faced by educators, particularly those in special education. I encourage teachers when they are struggling to seek support, acknowledge their struggles, and cultivate a supportive community so they can thrive.

This last school year, the district partnered with a university to create their own credentialing program where teachers work in a classroom with a master teacher, take classes for one year, and receive a teaching credential and a master's degree. They also get paid a stipend. Graduates also received priority hiring status. I worked within this program part-time as a practicum supervisor, observing and giving feedback to one new teacher.

All resident teachers in this program graduated in June. Soon, I will teach the second cohort of resident teachers a class on special education.

During the last week of school, I went to visit and congratulate the resident teacher I worked with all year. She worked in a special education middle school classroom. I had visited and observed the class all year, so the students knew me. I brought them cupcakes. As I passed out the cupcakes, one kiddo said, "Hey bracelet lady, you're back. I have bracelets too." He held up his arms to display a couple of beaded bracelets.

"I have seven on each hand for balance," I told him.

"Can I have one of yours, I want more bracelets," he said.

"Awww, these were gifts, but you never know what life has to offer," I said.

The day before the end of the year I walked in the classroom with a little cloth bag. The teachers smiled and nodded (I had emailed them) when I asked if I could have students come in and choose a beaded bracelet. Bracelet Boy nodded when I showed him the choices. He chose the one I thought he would like. His priceless smile made my day. He knew he was seen and valued. It takes a moment to do something kind for people. Always be kind. Lead with love.

Conscious Education

Unconscious bias refers to the attitudes, beliefs, and stereotypes that unconsciously influence our perceptions, decisions, and behavior toward others, often without our awareness. These biases can be shaped by various factors such as upbringing, socialization, media, and cultural norms.

Unconscious bias influences the way educators perceive and interact with students, particularly those from marginalized or underrepresented groups. In 2016, the district I currently work in began creating an unconscious bias workshop that focused on the experiences of our African American students. We rebranded it "Conscious Education" to highlight the positive nature of this work. I was part of a team of teachers who developed a three-day series. In 2023, we revised the workshops, honoring the original work but editing the curriculum based on district data and needs. The Conscious Education 1.0 workshop is now two days, and we also introduced a Conscious Education 2.0 workshop that lasts for one day. Recently, the district mandated that all staff members undergo the Conscious Education 1.0 training. Our workshops are now in high demand, and this beautiful work adds another layer to the social justice efforts required for our district to establish an anti-racist educational system.

The goal of the Conscious Education workshops is to assist all district staff in managing their biases, changing their behavior, and tracking their progress. The workshops challenge stereotypes and enable credentialed and classified staff to connect with one another and learn from experiences different from their own. There is still a long journey ahead for the education system to address inequity in schools. While structural changes to policies have occurred, as evidenced by our equity statement, we must enhance the diversity of our teaching and leadership staff. In California, approximately 23% of our student population is white, while 63% of the teacher population is white (EdSource, 2023).

Teachers have the opportunity to reach every student, every day. We must create safe spaces for learning and reconsider our mindset as teachers. We only know what we know, but once we know better, we must do better. Leading these workshops has changed the way I view others who have different lived experiences than mine.

Yesterday, we guided participants in examining their unconscious bias. I never thought I would be an unconscious bias trainer; then again, I never thought I would be a teacher. To examine our unconscious bias, participants engage in various exercises. One moment in the workshop stands out to me to this day. It was during the social geography exercise, where I spoke for five minutes with another person about my identity. Participants conversed in groups or with partners. While there were many questions related to identity, one stood out to me the most. "What groups/people were considered different by your family and/or community? (i.e., religion, race, class, sexual orientation, gender, etc.) How was the difference treated?" A trusted friend happened to be in the workshop with me, sitting at our table. At the time, I was not "out" as bisexual to district staff.

"So, I grew up being told that gay people were going to hell in the church. My dad used to make fun of gay men. It was a secret that my sister Barbara, who passed away when I was a teenager, had girlfriends. So when I started questioning my own identity, it was difficult. When I had a girlfriend in my twenties, we went to Pride in San Francisco. My dad saw my rainbow sticker with 'YES I AM' on my car window and scraped it off with a razor blade in front of me. 'No daughter of mine' resonated in my ears. Tears pooled in my eyes, and my voice shook. My friend listened as I spoke, nodding her head, not interrupting as instructed. When I finished, she said, "Thank you for being so brave." Then, she shared her social geography, and I listened, holding that sacred space. It was a pivotal moment in my life.

As a facilitator of this workshop on examining our unconscious bias, it's essential to share our own experiences. I felt a twinge of shame when I disclosed that I was a member of the LGBTQ+ community after the thirty attendees completed a quiz on their knowledge of LGBTQ+ terms. The next morning, I received an email from a participant thanking me for sharing my identity as a bisexual woman married to a man. I won't share their words, but I can share my reply.

> *Thank you for sharing your journey with me. It's funny; I still questioned if I should have shared about my sexuality until you sent this email. Thank you for being you, for being brave, and for helping me realize that we are not alone. You have a friend in me forever.*
>
> *In gratitude and solidarity,*
>
> *Jackie*

We may never fully grasp the impact of our Conscious Education workshops. If an adult felt like this, think of how our students feel in this system. Conscious Education enables us to unlearn shame, move past guilt, and work toward equity for all in the education system. By raising awareness of unconscious bias through workshops like Conscious Education, educators are encouraged to reflect on and challenge their own biases, fostering a more inclusive and equitable learning environment. Addressing unconscious bias is not only essential for promoting equity in education but also for fostering empathy, understanding, and connection among educators and students with diverse backgrounds and experiences. Most districts do not have mandatory unconscious bias training.

Remaining Teachable

Great teaching requires one to be a lifelong learner. One of the most challenging experiences in my educational career was completing my dissertation. I spent a year working with my committee chair, furiously writing without sleep. I always wrote, but my dissertation and doctoral degree instilled in me the work ethic necessary to finish a book. When I walked across that stage at graduation and heard myself called "Dr. Jacqueline Mantz," something within me was forever changed. I will always be Dr. Jacqueline Mantz. No one can take that away from me.

Teachers have private lives, and we all face challenges. It is not always acceptable to talk about them. Some of us are in recovery. I will always be an alcoholic. This is a fact for me, and I own it. Today, it is a gift. Nothing influences my day-to-day teaching career more than what I've learned in a different kind of room. I know there is something called anonymity in the program I practice and have practiced since August 22nd, 2009. I am no poster child for any twelve-step program. But the program has taught me to practice certain principles in all my affairs. The twelve spiritual principles of recovery are as follows: acceptance, hope, faith, courage, honesty, patience, humility, willingness, brotherly love, integrity, self-discipline, and service. My service commitment is on Sundays. I give out chips, tokens of success, for various lengths of sobriety. Today, a man received his one-year chip. When he walked up as we sang "Happy Birthday" to him, I put my hand on my heart when he shared his story. I remember my own one-year chip. It was one of the best days of my life.

The first time I saw a former student in the sobriety rooms, I felt my stomach clench. He looked at me, tipped his Dodgers cap, and said, "Don't worry, it's anonymous." I now internally giggle when I see a fellow teacher or former student in the program. If they see me, then I see them. Like teaching, in sobriety, I am a lifelong learner. I have a home group like students have a homeroom. My work with others includes being a sponsor to other women in the program. They say you have to give it away to keep it. So I keep it, my sobriety, the foundation of my life. But not everyone does, and this is the hardest part of living a life of sobriety. It is hard to watch people make choices and suffer the consequences. For those of us who are truly alcoholics, when we take that first drink, all bets are off. Many times people end up in jail, institutions, or dead. I have seen it all in my years in sobriety. Maybe this story in the book will help someone. If you need help, know that we are here. So let me tell you another story about friendship.

Ghost's Ink

We met at the 6 a.m. 559 meeting in Palm Springs, California. I was a couple of years sober when you walked into the rooms of A.A. You were one of those women men wanted to kiss and other women wanted to be; startlingly thin and tall with black hair cut in a Mia Wallace bob, Joan Didion cool. Your smile was slight, and your tattooed arched eyebrows said it all. "I am not supposed to be here." You had such style, lady. You were dressed like you were coming from an art show with black baggy pants and a loose tank top with a long, camel-colored sweater. I can still see those triangle golden and silver hoops shaking slightly as you identified as an alcoholic.

I don't remember the first time we had a conversation. But what I do remember are all the years of conversations about books, music, movies, and teaching. You and I shared a love of Didion. You even have a tattoo on your shoulder (I still want to copy it) written in typewriter font, "WE TELL OUR STORIES IN ORDER TO LIVE." You were the best friend I had dreamed of as a young girl. I always wanted someone to get me and for me to get them. Then you appeared in a run-down room that smelled like coffee. You didn't look like you belonged, but you were exactly where you were supposed to be and so was I. We sat in that room for years. After every meeting, we would tell one another our sick secrets, healing one another.

"Jackie, you know we're going to be those old broads who sit on the beach together with our saggy flesh and faded tattoos, right?" We were friends for years. I remember our trip to

Carpinteria. We had crossed the train tracks that day to get to the beach. We wrote our names in the sand and took pictures with the ocean and the salt and the sun, and it was perfect. That photo of the sand and our feet and the ocean sat on the counter in my beach-themed bedroom for years even as I tried not to look at it. The photo reminded me how this too shall pass. Forever, I thought we would be friends, forever until one day you were gone. I cried over and over for you, mourning our friendship which was ripped away from me suddenly. It's like Didion said, "Life changes fast. Life changes in the instant. You sit down to dinner and life as you know it ends." The end of our friendship was painful, an ache that never healed. Tears ran down my face in my bubble bath whenever I would reread *Slouching Towards Bethlehem*. What is it about loss that makes the formerly beautiful and sacred, painful and scarred?

I never thought until you that platonic love could break my heart. When I struggled for two years during Covid, you had already ghosted me. You didn't know that my Boston Terrier, Harper Lee, died at only five years old. I couldn't tell you how I wasn't sleeping, reading in the middle of the night, night after night. I didn't get to tell you how I had called a mental health hotline for help. The customer service representative was not helpful as he thought my dad had died rather than my dog. "My dog, D-O-G, died, not my dad. My dad died fifteen years ago," I screamed into the phone. I laughed hysterically alone in grief. Alone, that's how I felt without you. Why? Why didn't you text me back when I texted you? I left teaching, lost you, and felt all alone in that shared office at the district. I called you in Oceanside when Joe and I were on vacation. I was at the beach riding my bike, and Joe was relaxing with the dogs in the RV.

"How's it going?"

"It's fine."

"Is everything okay?"

"Why would you ask that? I'm fine."

"Is everything okay with you?"

"I'm okay too. What's going on? You don't seem to want to be around me anymore. I know you are mad about losing your teaching job, but that's not my fault. I'm sorry I still teach. Is that what's wrong?"

"Jackie, stop, just stop. I don't want to go over all that. How dare you throw it in my face. Everything is not about you." We went back and forth. I don't want to remember. All I remember was damage. The damage I did with my words. Years passed. I put you on my heart's shelf. Time, it took time to forgive you for forgetting me. Now I remember all the times you were there for me. You always listened whenever I cried about a fight Joe and I had had. You would take a long drag of your cigarette and laugh whenever I bitched about my twin sister. You gave me the gift of your friendship for years, so I decided to wish you well. Then I prayed for your well-being, every morning and every night on my knees. I found forgiveness the way I found sobriety, on my knees with the help of a power greater than myself. One day I spoke aloud to you as I sat in the bathtub, "Don't come back to me. Just live a beautiful life. Be sober and well, dear friend." Every time I read *The Year of Magical Thinking*, I thought of you. One day, a text appeared on my phone.

"Jackie, I am so sorry for not replying to your calls or texts. I do not deserve your forgiveness, but I am asking for it. I have been going through a lot. Would you meet me for coffee so we can talk?"

I texted back immediately. "Hey YOU, of course, I will meet you. Let me know where and when and I will be there." We met at Tony's Burgers. Over buffalo wings with extra sauce and ranch and small mini cheesy sliders, you told me, "I was drinking, Jackie. It wasn't you. I know I hurt you. I just couldn't be around you as I wasn't sober." I listened and listened some more. I held your shaking hand, the buffalo sauce like blood sealing our sisterhood. You cried and told me you needed help.

"I love you, no matter what." The years spent apart collapsed like sandcastles when the ocean waves hit them. This is love. I wanted you to stay sober after that day. Alcoholism is a cunning, baffling, and powerful disease. It lays to ruin some of the most beautiful souls I have ever met. But, all we have is today. Today you and I have matching camel tattoos on our right wrists. We don't have to drink today, I pray. But we do need to be friends, come what may.

What does this have to do with teaching? Trying to control everything and everyone is a waste of our energy. Accept people for who they are, and great events will come to pass within you. Focus on what you can control in life. Now I can see that that was why I was exhausted for so many years. The system tells me I must control kids, but kids will do what they do. It is up to us as teachers to put structures into place that allow for all students to learn. I treat every student like they are a newcomer. Show them love and empathy, get to know their stories, and tell them some of your own. This is why I love teaching more every day. Teaching is an act of love. But true teachers listen more than they talk. Nelson Mandela said, "I learned to have the patience to listen when people put forward their views..." This is how people learn from one another, by listening to others' words and stories. They will remember you. How do you want to be remembered?

The Dog's Way

It was love at first sight when I saw a little black-and-white fur ball crawling around on a blanket in West Covina in April of 2011. Joe got Elizabeth Barrett Browning (Lizzy) for me for our first-year anniversary gift after I lost my cat, Henry David Thoreau. I was sober for over a year and ready to have a dog. The word "dog" is such a simple word for such an immense being. Living with dogs has profoundly changed the essence of my life. They have taught me to live and appreciate the present and the simple act of living.

"Dog" spelled backward is "God." They are some of my best teachers. I want you to understand that teaching is connected to everything I do. For you to see me again as accurately as possible with all my wrinkles and cracks. Remember, this is how the light gets in. We all have our stories. We all have gifts and challenges. We are all human. Remember every student you teach has a story. Here is one day in my recent life. I am fifty-two years old, a teacher, sober, and my life is beautiful. But some days I still struggle. Plus, I had to include my dogs in this book as they have enriched my life with unconditional love.

Once upon a time not so long ago, I woke up to the sound of Lizzy snoring. She had stolen the blankets, again. Her pink belly rose and fell. I counted the rise and fall of her chest for one minute. Lizzy was almost thirteen years old and had a heart murmur. Every moment she took a breath was a gift. I looked at her belly and noticed one of her nipples was larger than usual. She had had numerous cancerous tumors removed the previous year. I enjoyed just gazing at Lizzy. Her black fur had turned to gray around her legs and muzzle. She had dandruff. But, her beauty mark was still on top of her head, a lovely imperfect circle. Lizzy began to lick my feet. I appreciated the grooming. She took such care of me. In return, I joyfully took care of her. Every week, I gave her and Sparrow baths. I loved my dogs to smell like lavender rather than like farm animals.

Sparrow lay between Joe and me. She was a little Boston Terrier ball of warmth. For a few minutes, I rested in the relaxation of the present moment. Then she farted, jumped up with wide eyes as if to ask, "Who did that?" Silent giggles overtook me. Sparrow came up to my face and stared at me. Joe was still asleep. It was 6:11 a.m. and time to go for a walk soon before I went to work.

We had gotten Sparrow in 2020, a few months after we lost Lizzy's best friend, Harper Lee. Harper Lee was also a Boston Terrier. No one could replace Harper Lee, as every loved one is irreplaceable. But caring for Sparrow allowed me to breathe through my grief after losing Harper Lee. Sparrow, like Harper Lee, was needy and a big baby. If I was home, she was next to me.

I walked my girls before I went to work. It gave me joy to watch them trot side by side. The moon was still in the sky. Orange and red curls appeared to the left of us. We walked the same path every day. Lizzy was slightly ahead of Sparrow. Lizzy stopped to sniff the bush and began to "backward sneeze," her chest heaving up and down. We stopped. This was why they wore harnesses when we walked, so I didn't pull on their necks because Lizzy had trouble breathing due to her heart issues. For a moment, I went into worry mode, but then I focused on the present moment. All we needed to do was walk. As long as we were together, all was well. Dogs do not wonder why or worry about the future, so I practiced being a dog at that moment.

We trotted down the block to the left. Many homes now had desert landscapes. Then we walked around the corner to houses with green grass. I had the clear plastic bag ready. We crossed the street to find more grass lawns. Lizzy pooped, and I saw blood in her fecal matter. Lizzy might need more blood tests. Recently, she had had her blood work done, and it had come back improved after we started her on a liver supplement. I would make a veterinarian appointment for Lizzy to check on her enlarged nipple and the blood in her poop. This is what we do for those we love.

Lizzy and Sparrow's hair raised on their backs as we saw and heard two little brown chihuahuas.

"Yap, yip, Yap, yip," the little dogs barked at us.

"Woof, growl, woof, growl," Lizzy replied as Sparrow cowered, lowering her head and whimpering. Lizzy had been attacked twice by dogs. She is our protector. My dogs are no mere pets. They are my spiritual compass. My fears drive me so often. Did I whimper, cower, bark, or take another path? Today, we all moved to the other side of the street. It was okay to walk away.

As I trotted Lizzy and Sparrow home now that Lizzy had found her pace, Harper Lee came to mind. I glanced up at the sky hoping for miracles. She had been Lizzy's little Boston Terrier buddy for a short five years. I remembered how sick she was that day at Banning Animal Hospital. How the doctor had said words I did not want to hear.

"She is not feeling well right now, and it will get worse. She has a headache, and her kidneys are shutting down. I would put her to sleep. Dogs cannot recover from kidney failure." I did not want to believe it; I wanted to put my hands over my ears, shut my eyes, and take her home so she could see her family one last time. But I knew I would not take her back. That moment I learned how true love could give one courage. We sat together for a few more moments, and tears silently fell down my cheeks as I whispered to her, "Come find me, Harper Lee." Then as I cradled her in my arms, she took her last breath. A few weeks later, I saw her outline in the sky as I glanced up into the heavens. Our loved ones are never destroyed, just undergoing metamorphosis.

The dogs and I finished our walk, and I said goodbye to my loved ones and went to work. When I got home from work, I was prepared to go out to dinner at the newly built Denny's. Joe and I argued about everything and nothing. At this moment, we both returned to the chaos of our childhoods. Our marriage is a work in progress, but at that moment, I could not remember to not react, to let the moment pass us by so I retorted. Joe retorted back, and tension filled the house. He took off in his car, saying he needed space. I didn't need space.

Why had we fought? I lay on the floor curled in a ball, crying. Would he come back? He always came back. This was Joe's way of coping, but it was not my way. I needed a hug. Lizzy and Sparrow felt my pain. They were my sweet willing comforters. We curled up on the dirty floor for sob-filled minutes. Finally, I got up on one elbow, sat up and into a cross-legged seated position, took three deep breaths, stood slowly up, and walked downstairs to the bedroom we called the blue room. It was ocean-themed with light, powder-blue walls and shells on the nightstand.

Lizzy and Sparrow were right beside me. I curled under the covers, grabbed my A.A. Book, read pages 64–67 that dealt with resentment, and took a breath in through my nose and out through my mouth. Lizzy curled up at my feet. Sparrow curled into my stomach. We were a pack of three without our alpha male, lonely but not alone, awaiting his return. Lizzy and Sparrow did not cry. They lay in silence. Their acceptance inspired me to breathe and ask God for peace. We heard the garage door opening, and we all sighed.

These last thirteen years in relationships with Lizzy, Harper Lee, and Sparrow have taught me the beauty and gifts of unconditional love. Love is acceptance of others with all their faults. Love is sitting with others in support during challenging times. Giving unconditional love is a gift in itself. What a relief to love without expectation. I strive to teach and live in a dog's way, but it is progress, not perfection. I am human. I struggle. But then, like I teach my students, I get up and never give up. When Joe walked in the door, Lizzy, Sparrow, and I were there to greet him.

"I'm sorry, Papa Bear, please forgive me," I whispered as I hugged Joe. Lizzy and Sparrow were standing beside us with their heads cocked as we hugged. He replied, "I'm sorry too, Mama Bear. I need to practice more patience."

Final Thoughts

Teaching is what I do best, so fame is not something I crave. My wistful wish is that you germinate a seedling of change after reading this book. The law of conservation of energy states that "Energy cannot be created or destroyed; it can only be changed from one form to another." Are you reading this book in prison? If you are, you probably read the other book I wrote with a friend, *Embracing Dawn: Two Women's Stories, Brought Together by the Prison Education Project* by Marie Rodriguez (my nom de plume) and Tessa McCarty (my student's nom de plume), which you can buy on Amazon. That one we completed in a year. I probably bought more copies to give away than they sold. But it does not matter. *Embracing Dawn* is up there in the ether. It lives, and I lived. This is enough for a writer like me.

In my free time, I read, write, exercise, eat, and hang out with Joe, Lizzy, and Sparrow. I am also a newbie to Apple TV, and we are currently binging *Ted Lasso.* I love the advice he gives to his players, "Be a goldfish." Goldfish have a ten-second memory. Let's not live in the past but learn from it. I survived my teenhood, years of alcoholic drinking, and two years as an administrator. If I have not told you, teaching, I love you. I love you from the tip of the curliest curl on my head to the bottom of my soles. I love you exactly as you are in this present moment. We are all imperfectly perfect. For instance, my feet are quite filthy as I walked on floors barefoot to write this morning. Yet, they got me here. Teaching is like dirty bare feet. It is best when you are down in the earth and muck with others' lived experiences.

Some of my best times have been spent in the classroom writing with kids. Their stories inspire me.

As a kid, I never thought I wanted to be a teacher. My childhood was chaotic and wild. I occasionally thought of what I wanted to be when I grew up. Roger Ebert, the film critic, filled my mind's eye. Roger Ebert was a strange idol for a young girl. My father loved movies and television. He would take us to see cinematic masterpieces like *Superman*, *Poltergeist*, and *Star Wars* at the Mission Tiki Drive-In every Saturday night. Roger Ebert and Gene Siskel were both movie reviewers for newspapers and the hosts of *At the Movies*, a Saturday morning television series that helped popularize film reviewing. They made a show out of verbally sparring while discussing films. A "two thumbs up" was like a restaurant receiving a Michelin Star. Ebert was the everyman movie reviewer whose humanity and humor poured out of him to counteract the pompous, elitist Siskel. Ebert could admit to liking a movie for being creative, goofy, or even bizarre. Within this cuddly man was a fine mind. In 1975, Ebert became the first film critic to win the Pulitzer Prize for criticism. He was one of my first teachers. Roger Ebert loved movies and wrote about them with reverence, humor, and respect. He taught me to think more deeply about movies and showed me the power of living a life of meaning. I did not become a movie critic, but I found a way to use my imagination, and my love of stories and writing, to grow the next generation of dreamers.

I started writing stories about my teaching experiences when I first got sober in 2009. I began working on writing a book about teaching when I returned to teaching in 2021. There have been changes to my teaching assignment. I no longer teach history. Although I enjoyed the experience, teaching reading and writing is my passion. Now I teach a daily creative writing class in addition to the weekly elective literary journal. This allowed me to expand the literary journal's scope. More students now submit pieces as they work on them in our creative writing class. Our third volume of *Third Eye Writings* debuted in December 2023. The theme was love and struggle. We published volume four of the literary journal in May of 2024, and the theme was identity. I hope to continue to curate students' writing as long as I teach at our school.

Thanks to going back to school virtually to get a yoga and social-emotional learning certification through Breathe for Change, my principal provided me with the opportunity to teach P.E. yoga. Only at a continuation school is one able to teach outside their credentialed area due to the smaller teaching staff. Yoga class is a time for us to calm our minds, stretch our bodies with our breath, and relax. It has been life-changing for students and for me. Doing yoga in a group is more beneficial as the energy can be felt in the room. I know students love savasana. This summer I signed up for a two-week, in-person yoga certification and retreat in Joshua Tree to further my knowledge. Due to this, I am working on giving up meat, as at the retreat, I will only have access to vegetarian meals. Letting go of eating meat is another step in my evolution as a human being. What I am trying to say here is that we are always growing and changing. I hope the stories you read here have allowed you to gain more empathy and compassion for students, teachers, and yourself. Remember, like RuPaul says, "If you can't love yourself, how in the hell are you gonna love somebody else?"

As a lifelong educator, I have seen so much triumph and tragedy in our educational world. These last four years back in the classroom have been the best years of my teaching career. I finally got it. We are here not to control but to inspire. We are here to listen as well as to speak. Not only that, but we are all on the journey together. At this moment in time, we are not together as a society on how to support all students in our educational system. This book is but my small part in bringing all teachers, students, administrators, parents, community members, and society into the conversation. May you read these stories and understand that all students are capable of learning, growing, and becoming brave stewards of our sacred planet.

May my journey help you understand how to live your best teaching life. The best teachers are those who dare to put their best authentic selves forward minute by minute, hour by hour, and year after year. For every success, there is a regret. For every opening, there is a closing. I have grown softer rather than harder as a teacher. Recently, I crave time more than money so I have let go of additional duties for next school year. I need time. Time to be with my beloved family. Time to spend working on my sobriety, writing, doing yoga, swimming, and traveling. I wish you all the gift of time doing what you love. May you all be well, free from suffering, and be as happy as it is possible to be during these tumultuous times. The light in me bows to the light in you.

Acknowledgments

I would like to thank but a few of the many people that helped me birth this book. Thank you, Mom and Dad, for loving me. The greatest gift you gave me is the knowledge that we are here to love and be loved. Joe, my *por vida* and true blue, thank you for loving me and for allowing me to love you. Roberta, you always inspired me to be the light I wish to see in the world. You are always and forever my big sis. Juanita, you are an inspiration as a writer. Annette, thank you for always being supportive and being the best mom ever to your children. I have so much gratitude for the Inlandia writing workshop writers who read all my drafts of these stories and gave me invaluable input. Vic, you are a gifted workshop leader, an amazing writer, and a light of a human being. Frances, your lovely spirit and home sustained me through the editing process. We worked so well together, and your book and my book are siblings. Thank you to Cati Porter and Mark Givens for all your support during all phases of the publishing process. I learned so much in the 909 Books Collective. May I continue to support all burgeoning writers, paying it forward. Finally, to my dogs, Lizzy, Harper Lee, and Sparrow; my own metaphorical tail is wagging in love for you!

In gratitude,

Dr. Jacqueline Marie Mantz Rodriguez

Works Cited

Alcoholics Anonymous. Alcoholics Anonymous World Services, 1939, p. 83.

California, State of. *Education Code*. 2018, leginfo.legislature.ca.gov/faces/codes_displaySection.xhtml?sectionNum=49005.4.&lawCode=EDC.

"CALPADS Primary Disability Category Codes." *California Department of Education.*, www.cde.ca.gov/ta/tg/ca/disablecodes.asp "Emotional disturbance (ED)" Accessed 8 June 2024.

CAST. "About Universal Design for Learning." *CAST*, 2018, www.cast.org/impact/universal-design-for-learning-udl. Accessed 17 July 2024.

Coates, Ta-Nehisi. *Between the World and Me*. New York, Spiegel & Grau, 14 July 2015.

Emery, Debra W., and Brian Vandenberg. "Special Education Teacher Burnout and ACT." *International Journal of Special Education*, vol. 25, no. 3, 2010, pp. 119–131.

Gruwell, Erin. *The Freedom Writers Diary*. Broadway Books/ New York, 1999.

Jerry Maguire. Directed by Cameron Crowe, TriStar Pictures, 1996.

King, Stephen. *Rita Hayworth and Shawshank Redemption*. Signet, 1982.

Lee, Yeunjoo, et al. "Perils to Self-Efficacy Perceptions and Teacher-Preparation Quality among Special Education Intern Teachers." *Teacher Education Quarterly* (Claremont, Calif.), vol. 38, no. 2, 22 Mar. 2011, pp. 61–76. Accessed 5 Aug. 2025.

Mccourt, Frank. *Angela's Ashes.* Scribner, 1996.

Mills, Janet. "The Track of Love & the Track of Fear." *The Four Agreements*, 16 Nov. 2019, www.thefouragreements.com/the-track-of-love-the-track-of-fear/. Accessed 10 June 2024.

Mills, Janet, and don Miguel Ruiz. "The Fourth Agreement: Always Do Your Best." *The Four Agreements*, 16 Nov. 2019, www.thefouragreements.com/the-fourth-agreement/. Accessed 17 July 2024.

The Shawshank Redemption. Directed by Frank Darabont, Warner Bros., 1994.

Vygotsky, L. S. *Mind in Society: The Development of Higher Psychological Processes.* Cambridge, Harvard University Press, 1978.

White, E.B. *Charlotte's Web.* Harper & Brothers, 1952.

Wynne, Martha Ellen, et al. "Adult Outcomes for Children and Adolescents with EBD." *SAGE Open*, vol. 3, no. 1, 6 Mar. 2013, p. 215824401348313, DOI: 0.1177/2158244013483133.

About the Author

Dr. Jacqueline Mantz Rodriguez became a teacher through providence. Jacqueline nearly dropped out of high school but graduated with the support of her family and teachers. She returned to college at the age of twenty-four after a mentor and peace officer told her she had potential. Jacqueline has a B.A. In English, two Master's degrees, and an Educational Doctorate. Jacqueline has worked within the education system for over twenty-four years in many different settings including non-public schools, special education, an online blended learning school, and now at a continuation high school. Jacqueline's philosophy of education is that teaching is an act of love and courage. Her ability to see every student as a fellow capable soul helps her facilitate student learning in a caring way that changes lives. Jacqueline was a District Teacher of the Year in 2022.

Jacqueline also volunteers for the Prison Education Project (PEP) teaching courses within the prison system. She co-wrote a book with a woman currently incarcerated titled *Embracing Dawn* under her pen name Marie Rodriguez. Jacqueline's writings have been published in various literary journals including the *Inlandia Literary Journal*, the *California English Journal*, and *Voices de la Luna Literary Journal.* She also was a contributor to the *UnPrison Project* blog located at https://unprison.org/up-blog.

THE 909 BOOKS COLLECTIVE

909 Books is an independent publisher with the experience of two leading regionally-based publishers behind it. **The 909 Books Collective** is a unique mentorship model that relies on its members to ensure mutual success. The exclusivity and vetting of authors/members ensures that all 909 Books publications meet the highest standards of book publishing.

WWW.909BOOKS.COM

www.ingramcontent.com/pod-product-compliance
Lightning Source LLC
LaVergne TN
LVHW091123080826
845145LV00008B/2023